Railroading The Back of Beyond

The Story of the Historic Murphy Branch Now Known As

THE GREAT SMOKY MOUNTAINS RAILWAY

The Route of the Asheville Cannonball and Cowee Tunnel

By *Mead Parce*
Mead Parce

Copyright © 1997

Harmon Den Press, Inc.
221 Ewbank Drive, Hendersonville, N.C. 28791

Railroad Through The Back of Beyond

The Story of the Historic Murphy Branch
Now Known as

THE GREAT SMOKY MOUNTAINS RAILWAY

The Route of the Asheville Cannonball and Cowee Tunnel

By Mead Parce

Copyright © 1997 by Mead Parce
All Rights Reserved.

No part of this book may be reproduced or transmitted in any form or by any means, electronic or mechanical, including photocopying, recording or by any information storage and retrieval system without prior written permission from the author except for the inclusion of brief quotations in a review.

Published by Harmon Den Press
221 Ewbank Drive
Hendersonville, NC 28791

Printed in the U.S.A.
Faith Printing Co.
Taylors, SC

Cover Design by Deron Edwards
Book Design by Mead Parce
Illustrations by Philip Van Pelt & James Killian Spratt

ISBN 0-9057461-1-9

Softcover

First Edition

The "Asheville Cannonball"

For Jessica, Matthew and Logan

Table of Contents

Preface 1
Introduction 3
Illustrations 5
Maps 9

Chapter I
In the Beginning Were Hopes and Dreams 11

Chapter II
Building the Railroad 23

Chapter III
Is the Cowee Tunnel Cursed? 37

Chapter IV
Southern's Murphy Branch 43

Chapter V
The Great Smoky Mountains Railway 59

Chapter VI
The Feeder Lines 73

Chapter VII
Railroaders' Memories 77

Chapter VIII
Three Outstanding Railroaders 87

Chapter IX
  A Mountain Man Remembers 103
Chapter X
  The Western North Carolina Railroad — Epilogue 109

Acknowledgements 111

Sources 115

Bibliography 115

Interviews 115

Index 117

Preface

This book is a "partial" history of the Western North Carolina railroad west of Asheville. Once called the "Murphy Branch," it is now The Great Smoky Mountains Railway. Why a "partial" history?

Two reasons: 1. It would take two or more volumes to record all of the history involving the Murphy Branch; 2. All history is ongoing and the final chapter of The Great Smoky Mountains Railway hasn't been lived yet, much less written.

This is not a technical book. It is written for those who would like to know more about the history of a time and place in their lives, even though it may be merely an excursion train trip.

For others, the book is a starting point in their own research into the history, lore and legend of the Murphy Branch. Others may find the book's value in the stories of people and places who were quite real in an earlier time.

This railroad is a key link in the cultural and economic heritage of the Western North Carolina mountains and its people. It ended the isolation of the "Hinterlands" of the Great Smokies. It gave the people of the "Back of Beyond" opportunity.

Recording an obscure railroad's opening up of a frontier, a last frontier in America, became a labor of love soon into the project.

When a friend, Gil Crouch, suggested a book on the Murphy Branch, now The Great Smoky Mountains Railway, I undertook the project because I strongly believe that future generations of mountain residents must know the region's cultural history to appreciate and enjoy the privilege of living and visiting in the mountains.

For those who love railroads and want another trip down memory lane, may you enjoy the trip as well. All aboard!

Typical Station

Introduction

Railroads are part of the American psyche for a number of reasons. The most compelling reason, perhaps, is the fact railroads opened our frontiers in both reality and symbolism.

Our rails west conquered the Western Frontier. Our rails south joined a sundered nation and opened the frontier of the New South.

The "Murphy Branch" opened the frontier of Western North Carolina in the 1890's, more than three decades after the East and West coasts were joined by rails across the western plains.

While it operated under different names - The Western North Carolina Railroad, Richmond & Danville, Southern Railway System, Norfolk Southern and now The Great Smoky Mountains Railway, its mission has been the same - transportation into and out of the mountains.

It has survived floods, landslides, war, economic decline, destruction of the great forests around it, relocation of the people it served, a giant dam, lake, four-lane highways and the coming of the automobile and truck.

Called "temporary" by its builder, it is still around.

Visitors to Western North Carolina derisively called its passenger trains "The Cannonball" because of their 15-miles-an-hour speed.

One Chicagoan called the railroad, "Two streaks of rust and a right-of-way."

Gone are the famous "hotel" or "candy" trains of yesteryear on other railroads. The Murphy Branch had no "candy" or "varnish." Its equipment was ancient and decrepit even in its heyday. But it still had glamour and excitement for those who rode its cars and rail. For those who lived in the splendid isolation of the Great Smokies, Nantahala and Balsam mountain ranges, the trip to Asheville aboard one of the four trains a day was as if they had been transported to New York, Washington or Philadelphia aboard a magic carpet.

While passenger service to most places in the nation is little or nonexistent today, the Murphy presently serves 184,401 rail passengers a year who want to ride an excursion train to relive or see for a first time the era of the American passenger railroad.

Shippers along the line receive freight service for bulk cargo in a high tech era.

By design, The Great Smoky Mountains Railway has recaptured the flavor of all railroading by including in its trains cars and engines from many railroads. A consist may include a steam engine, a diesel-electric engine, baggage car from the 1930's, passenger coaches, dining cars, open air cars and even a caboose with the famous "doghouse" roof. There is something for everyone.

The railway has brought back the fun of rail travel. It has history, scenery, a river to forever, beautiful mountains, tunnels, lake, long bridge, old stations, flag stops, steep grades and some of the finest whitewater kayaking in the world along its route.

And its whistles still go "woooo...woooo" as part of past, present and future.

This book is about the railroad, its history.

Illustrations

Title Page - A 1911 Mikado used by Southern Railway during the heyday of passenger traffic.

Frontispiece - The "Asheville Cannonball."

Chapter I - An early wood-burning engine of the type first used on the Western North Carolina Railroad and the Richmond & Danville, early owners of the line.

Chapter II - A classic trestle as built on both the main line and logging railroads in the mountains. Hawksnest Trestle and others were built on the same lines by Will Sandlin Jr. Sandlin built a trestle of this design in the Snowbird Mountains for a logging line after working for the Richmond & Danville. A "Climax" engine used in logging in the mountains is at the end of the chapter.

Chapter III - This is a symbolic drawing of a train coming out of the Cowee Tunnel. This is where 19 workers died while trying to cross the Tuckasegee River on their way to work on the tunnel.

Opposite - Drawing of a Southern steam engine and train thundering out of the Cowee Tunnel and crossing the Tuckasegee River on a steel bridge that is still in use today. This is where present-day Great Smoky Mountains Railway trains cross the Tuckasegee just before entering the tunnel.

Chapter IV - This a drawing of an actual double-header on Southern Railways in the 1940's when steam engines needed helpers or double-headers to cross Balsam Gap and climb Nantahala Gorge from Wesser to Topton.

Chapter V - The Great Smoky Mountains Railway Consolidated steam engine No. 1702, a former military railway engine built during World War II.

Chapter VI - Drawing of a Shay engine used on logging railroads in the Great Smokies and Plott Balsams to bring out logs to Southern's junction and shipment to sawmills. The Shay, Heisler and Climax logging engines were gear driven, thus giving them greater power for steep climbs into the mountains. At the end of the chapter is a drawing of a helper engine from Andrews backing down Nantahala grade at the Hawksnest fill. The fill replaced the trestle built by Will Sandlin Jr. There is a graveyard near the fill where convicts who died in the terrible winter of 1885 are buried.

Chapter VII - The Asheville Cannonball, called that by "outlanders" because the train's speed of 15-miles-per-hour was so slow. Engineer Gene Adams operated a steam engine similar to this one with a train of one baggage car and coach. At one time the line had four passenger trains a day such as this one. The train is crossing one of the trestles along the line from Asheville to Murphy because of the many creeks in the mountains.

Chapter VII also has a drawing of a typical station agent's office such as was used by Harold Hall when he began with the railroad, and his uncle, C.O. Hall, who retired as the last agent at Andrews. The agents sold tickets, handled freight and operated the telegraph. Station agents were important people in the railroad structure.

One of the stories in Chapter VII is about engineer James Fox putting water in the tender tank. Many stations along the line had wooden water tanks. The huge arm could fill an engine's tender very rapidly via gravity flow from the tank. The term "tank town" came from the various small towns in America that had water tanks but little else. "Tank town" is a derisive term.

Chapter VIII - A builder's drawing of a Consolidations steam engine of the type used on Southern Railways in earlier days. The Consolidations had two wheels at the front and eight drivers. This is called 2-8-0.

Chapter IX - A typical Southern Railway consist of steam engine, baggage car and coach making its way along the right-of-way that is no longer "two streaks of rust." Southern upgraded the track in the early 1900's.

Chapter X - A modern freight train on The Great Smoky Mountains Railway.

Ritter Lumber Mill at Proctor

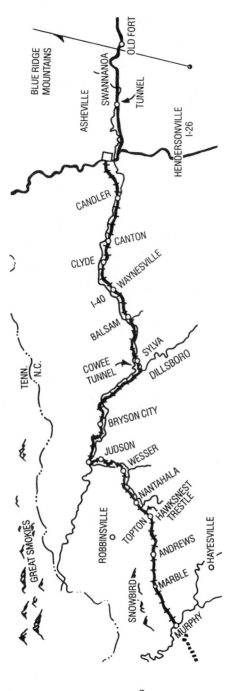

Map No. 1 - The Western North Carolina Railroad (Murphy Branch) before the construction of Lake Fontana in 1944. The rail line ran from Asheville in the east to Murphy in the west.

Map No. 2 - The present Great Smoky Mountains Railway runs from Dillsboro to Andrews. The track from Andrews to Murphy has been pulled up. Eastward from Dillsboro the track is owned and operated by Norfolk Southern. Lake Fontana is the dark area just beyond Bryson City and Judson. The area just north of the lake is part of the Great Smoky National park. It is called "North Shore" and is accessible only by boat from the south shore of the lake. The North Shore is a area where the logging towns on Noland and Hazel creeks were located. Logging railroads served the area.

Chapter I

Highballin'

In the Beginning Were Hopes and Dreams

When the Western North Carolina Railroad opened the frontier of Western North Carolina, it fulfilled the dreams of a people shut off by towering mountain ranges from the rest of civilization even if it did not quite fulfill the hopes of the men who dreamed of joining the East and West with twin ribbons of iron and steel through Western North Carolina.

The railroad was called the greatest industrial event in the history of Western North Carolina when it was completed.

It still is.

The idea for a railroad through Western North Carolina's mountains to the Midwest first came up in 1822 when Dr. John Caldwell, president of the University of North Carolina, extolled the merits of a possible railroad from Beaufort on the coast to Asheville in the mountains. Dr. Caldwell was well read on the future of rail travel despite the fact the first steam engines to run on track were just in the developmental stage.

The suggestion came up again in 1827 when South Carolina's Joel Poinsett of Charleston suggested a railroad from Charleston through the Blue Ridge Mountains to Tennessee and thence to the Ohio Valley. Poinsett, for whom the Poinsettia plant is named and a businessman-diplomat, envisioned trade between the port city of Charleston and the Midwest just as Dr. Caldwell envisioned trade from Beaufort to Asheville and beyond. In fact, in 1833 Poinsett published a pamphlet advocating such a railroad.

Judge Mitchell King of Flat Rock, a Charlestonian who summered in the mountains of Henderson County, was a strong advocate of a railroad as were businessmen in Tennessee who proposed connecting rails from that state with a proposed Western North Carolina railroad.

Two other major proponents of a railroad were Robert Y. Hayne and James Bennett, both South Carolina businessmen.

Historian James Mooney says Col. William H. Thomas, white chief of the Cherokee, is the father of the railroad through Western North Carolina. According to Mooney, Thomas, elected to the N.C. General Assembly in 1848, pushed for a series of road improvements for Western North Carolina that included a railroad to develop the copper mines at Ducktown, Tn., beyond Murphy.

Another idea was to connect at Paint Rock on the French Broad River north of Asheville.

Thus, a railroad through the mountains had its beginning or genesis in the dream of rails linking North Carolina, Tennessee and the Midwest.

Unfortunately, a great deal of time often elapses between an idea and actuality. In the case of the "Murphy Branch," the name given it by its builders, it would be years before steam engines would huff and chuff through the Great Smokies.

It took a long time to overcome the lack of money, as well as cope with embezzlement, fraud, bankruptcies, impassable mountains, rivers, floods, landslides, Civil War and the political battles of a divided land and state.

In the end the Murphy Branch was built, but not before a lot of men died in construction accidents; others became heroes and others, labeled crooks.

In its history, the Murphy Branch has been part of a number of railroads. Today it is The Great Smoky Mountains Railway, an amazing story of revival in the annals of railroading.

While Joel Poinsett wrote about his dream in 1833, it wasn't until 1852 that North Carolina's General Assembly chartered a Western North Carolina railroad. It was to be capitalized at $3 million, financed two-thirds by state funds and the remaining third by counties and individuals.

To North Carolina's leading citizens, it was deemed important that a link be made with rail lines proposed from Cincinnati to Paint Rock on the Tennessee-North Carolina state line north of Asheville. While North Carolina was a year ahead in its planning, Tennessee was not far behind. In 1853 the state chartered a railroad to run from Ohio through Kentucky and Tennessee to Paint Rock, N.C.

The Paint Rock route was good, but the engineers decided a second route should be built. Thus, the North Carolina General Assembly issued a second charter, this time in 1855, for a route from Asheville through the valley of the Pigeon and Tuckasegee rivers to connect with a proposed Blue Ridge Railroad on the Tennessee River in the far western part of the state.

There were high hopes in the mountains of Western North Carolina that the region's isolation might end with the coming of the iron horse. Without a railroad, there was little hope for business, travel, and industry because the terrain was difficult for the other kind of horse. Yes, there were main roads through gaps in the mountains, and even turnpikes, actually old Buffalo and Indian trails widened by long usage to allow the passage of stagecoaches and wagons.

Away from the turnpikes and main roads, the other routes were little more than foot trails into coves and hollows. The mountain people had no way to get their crops to market.

The drovers of Tennessee took months to herd their cattle and flocks of turkeys through the mountains to markets in South Carolina on what have been called the "oft traveled roads."

This is why hopes were high and the idea of a railroad had great support in the mountains.

The chartering of the Western North Carolina Railroad in 1852 to run from Salisbury to Asheville came just four years after Gov. John Motley Morehead, considered by many historians as the man who took the dreams of others and made them come to reality, began to push the need for a railroad. Morehead became governor in 1841 and immediately asked the General Assembly to approve a plan for transportation beyond anything in the state. It would consist of railroads, canals and turnpikes.

Gov. Morehead left office in 1845 without seeing his "North Carolina Plan" approved. However, he didn't give up. Upon leaving office, he began to travel the state preaching the need for railroads to serve the public. Everybody agreed, but nobody did anything.

It took a romance to get everybody's attention. U.S. Sen. Stephen Douglas, famous for his senatorial campaign debates with Abraham Lincoln, traveled to North Carolina to court a woman he had met. The roads were terrible and the silver-tongued senator from Illinois said so every chance he got.

His theory: North Carolina needed railroads to escape the backwardness and isolation that gripped the state.

Historians also note that Dorothea Dix, the famous reformer, also found North Carolina's roads without a single redeeming feature.

The result is former Gov. Morehead sent a bill to the General Assembly that passed by one vote when a Jacksonian Democrat went against his own party and voted the needs of his district. Calvin Graves, presiding officer of the Senate, when he broke a tie vote in favor of the railroad, had committed political suicide. He never held public office again.

However, his vote began an era of development that continues today.

Morehead set out to raise $1 million and did. With the goal reached, he became president of the North Carolina Railroad and builder of the line. The line from Goldsboro to Charlotte was completed in January 1856. Morehead resigned soon after completion of the line to promote the eastern extension to the coast and the western extension to Asheville and beyond.

Work began in 1855 on the track from Salisbury to Asheville. A financial panic in 1857 delayed construction. In 1861, the eve of the Civil War, work was halted two miles east of Morganton.

The enterprise was engulfed by a national crisis - the Civil War. It would be four long and bloody years before the idea of a railroad to the Midwest and beyond could be resurrected.

While the Civil War was a tragedy for the country, it was a major disaster in Western North Carolina for it pitted brother against brother and family against family in the worst guerrilla warfare seen in this country. This guerrilla warfare, later extending into the political arena in North Carolina, hampered efforts to extend the railroad through the mountains and set the stage for fraud by carpetbaggers in financing postwar construction.

The North Carolina Railroad from Salisbury to Charlotte and the Richmond & Danville Railroad were damaged in the waning days of the war when Union Gen. George Stoneman led a raid into Southeastern Virginia and Western North Carolina in an effort to destroy railroads and release Union prisoners being held at Salisbury. It turned out the prisoners had been moved before Stoneman arrived.

Stoneman's raiders were successful in cutting two railroads, destroying track, rolling stock and depots. He also came within a half hour of capturing Confederate President Jefferson Davis and his cabinet, all of whom were fleeing south through North Carolina. Stoneman's Raiders later took part in the chase through South Carolina and into Georgia, where Davis and his aides were captured in the latter state.

It is part of the lore of the mountains that Davis and the cabinet once considered Flat Rock, called "Little Charleston in the Mountains," in Henderson County below Asheville, a possible site for the Confederate government when it was forced out of Richmond by Union Gen. U.S. Grant's armies.

Christopher Memminger, former secretary of the Treasury for the Confederacy, lived in Flat Rock, and the mountain hamlet was considered by some officials in Richmond a safe place. Actually, Henderson County was divided equally by Union and Confederate sympathizers and was anything but safe. The idea died aborning.

Cpl. William P. Turner, an 18-year-old Union cavalryman with the 12th Ohio, remembered years later the tearing up of Richmond & Danville track during his unit's march to Winston-Salem. He wrote in his memoirs about Gen. Stoneman's telegrapher in Christiansburg, Va., getting on line with a Confederate telegrapher in Lynchburg and "talking" before the Lynchburg telegrapher "caught on." Turner also told of being with a unit of the 12th Ohio cavalry that tricked Confederate guards of the Catawba River bridge near Morganton into surrendering by bluffing they were part of a large Union force. The Union troopers burned the bridge as Confederate cavalry rode up to the other side. It was too late.

Damage to the railroad during the war amounted to $111,000, based on prewar prices for material and labor. The other interesting part is the railroad had no debt. However, it didn't have much track or rolling stock left either. In 1866, the rolling stock consisted of five engines, three passenger coaches, two mail cars, 12 flatcars and five boxcars.

With the war over, North Carolina's leading citizens turned to rehabilitating its railroads. The first priority of the Western North Carolina Railroad was to complete the line to Morganton, a few miles beyond where construction had stopped when the war began. The second priority was to extend the road into Western North Carolina. Trackage to Morganton was completed soon after the end of the war in 1865.

About this time more money was needed to complete the railroad to Asheville, but there wasn't any, so the General Assembly voted to issue bonds for completion of the railroad to its points west.

Unfortunately, there weren't many buyers of the bonds. First, money was scarce in North Carolina after the Civil War. Second, those who did have money didn't have much faith in the state's ability to repay the bonds because tax revenues were so slim in the postwar period.

Corruption and politics also entered into the problem. Whigs and Democrats were leaders of state government before the Civil War; but, if they had joined and fought for the Confederacy, they could not hold office until they took an oath to uphold the Union.

After the war, North Carolina residents elected Raleigh newspaper editor and publisher, W.W. Holden, governor. He was a Whig turned Democrat turned Republican who opposed continuation of the Civil War after the Confederate defeat at Gettysburg, saying the cause was lost. He was named provisional governor as a Republican by President Andrew Johnson, a native of North Carolina. President Johnson, interestingly enough, was elected vice-president as a Democrat on the ticket with Republican President Abraham Lincoln. Johnson became president when Lincoln was assassinated. Holden had backed Zeb Vance of Asheville for governor and then opposed him after the war, winning the election on his own.

Haw River and Raleigh banker George Swepson was president of the Western North Carolina Railroad right after the war.

Getting a bond issue for the railroad through the General Assembly was a tough sell, so Swepson hired former Union Gen. Milton S. Littlefield to bribe lawmakers and obtain passage of the bonds.

It worked. Littlefield, a friend of President Abraham Lincoln from the days he helped swing the Illinois delegation to Lincoln before the 1861 Republican nominating convention, commanded a company of infantry at the beginning of the war, fought at Shiloh, became assistant provost marshal in Memphis, recruited former slaves for Union ranks in South Carolina, and commanded the sea islands of South Carolina from his headquarters at Hilton Head when he accepted the surrender of Charleston, S.C., after the collapse of the Confederacy and Union Gen. William T. Sherman's march through Georgia.

Littlefield came by his credentials honestly - born in Upstate New York of good stock; lived near Syracuse, a hotbed of abolition activity which no young man could fail to notice; moved to Grand Rapids, Mich., where he taught school; became a sergeant in the Grand Rapids Light Guards Militia. Grand Rapids also was the place where the Republican Party flourished with missionary zeal. Littlefield joined the party and then moved to Jerseyville, Ill., where he went into business. He got his brother a job as a lawyer in the office of Herndon and Lincoln in Springfield, Ill., the capital.

It was at a time when the railroads were being built to the West. Historians of that era note the enabling legislation was often written by railroad lawyers, bonds canvassed by financiers and then sent to state legislatures for approval.

Proponents of the bills were not above bribery to get their way. Littlefield learned lessons on how to reach legislators that would stand him in good stead in North Carolina as Swepson's agent.

Gen. Littlefield would become the "Prince of Carpetbaggers" and Swepson a "scalawag" in the Reconstruction era.

A carpetbagger was a fellow from the North who saw opportunity in the South after the Civil War just as many Confederate officers and men saw opportunity in the West. He arrived with little more than a carpetbag (a suitcase made of carpet) holding his worldly goods. A "scalawag," on the other hand, was a native Southerner who worked with the Freedman's Bureau and supported Republican efforts after the war to gain control of the various legislatures and become a political leader. Scalawags saw their main chance for wealth and power amid the chaos that is the aftermath of war. They joined the winners.

Swepson came under fire as president of the Western North Carolina Railroad when no work was being done on building the roadbed to the west so he named Littlefield as president of the line. The two men took the bonds approved by the General Assembly, sold some, paid off legislators with some and used others to buy three railroads in Florida. The idea was to control not only the Western North Carolina Railroad but also build a railroad empire in Florida, a state that, too, was trying to rebuild with a carpetbag government.

When dust settled, both men were on the run, Littlefield in New York, and Swepson in New Jersey. Swepson offered to pay back some of the $4 million stolen from the railroad and state. He did and wound up one of the more prosperous bankers in Raleigh during his later years. One of the beneficiaries of his largesse was Raleigh's First Baptist Church of which his wife was a leading member. They lived next door.

Gen. Littlefield offered to return to North Carolina if all those state officials and businessmen involved with him stood trial along with him. It is said the state official sent to New York to negotiate Littlefield's return reviewed the Union general's record of payments and deals. After two hours the official told the general he would not be asked to return to stand trial. Too many Tar Heel businessmen and legislators had aided Swepson and Littlefield in their scam and received bonds for their efforts.

The state decided to move forward rather than prosecute.

Raleigh newspaper editor and publisher Jonathan Daniels, author of a book about Gen. Littlefield called *Prince of the Carpetbaggers*, was not as harsh as some historians toward Littlefield. He suggested that Littlefield actually might have been a railroad speculator along with Swepson and they used the same strategy as Jim Fisk, Jay Gould, Collis P. Huntington and others in railroad speculation as a means to an end but lost in the shaky financial markets of the times. There is some merit to the theory since all of the southern railroads nearly collapsed at one time or another only to be bailed out and reorganized by the major financial houses of New York, the place where the money had to come from in rebuilding the South after the war.

The railroad went into receivership and into state ownership before work to Asheville would resume.

With the scandal of the Prince of Carpetbaggers and dozens of scalawags dormant, efforts to get a railroad to the Midwest went forward, but not without politics as Union Republicans and Confederate Democrats fought it out in Raleigh.

Finally, a deal was struck to obtain more money to build the railroad after nothing had been done during the Swepson-Littlefield era and thereafter.

Democrats in the eastern part of the state agreed to support a bill calling for $850,000 in new bonds to pay off creditors and complete the railroad if Democrats in the west would support a bill calling for a constitutional convention to end the election of county commissioners and justices of the peace, a process that had led to carpetbag government after the Civil War. Under the bill the General Assembly would choose commissioners and the justices. The bill's intent was to end the election of Blacks in North Carolina's eastern counties where former slaves were in a majority.

The bill passed in 1875 after much wrangling, and in 1877 Democrats took back state government with the election of former Gov.

Zebulon Vance to another term as governor, his second trip to the governor's mansion in Raleigh.

With Vance's election, work began on the rails up the Blue Ridge escarpment from Old Fort to Asheville the same year. Construction of this section of the railroad is an epic of railroad building in the United States.

Vance installed Maj. James Wilson, one of the prewar contractors of the line, as president, superintendent and chief civil engineer. He, in turn, hired Col. Thad Coleman as his chief assistant.

Convict labor was assigned the task of building the roadbed. It was how public works got done. Five hundred Black convicts were assigned to the building of the railroad with picks, shovels and drag pans. It is one of the shameful chapters in the building of the railroad.

Conditions in the labor camps were described as "wretched" by those who visited the sites despite what doctors assigned the camps said about conditions. The convicts were dressed in yellow and black-striped garb, fed food from open fires, and put into fetid, airless boxcars for sleeping at night.

Official records indicate 150 convicts lost their lives in the construction of the railroad while the unofficial count lists 400 deaths. When a convict died on the job, he was buried beside the track under construction without ceremony. A number of convicts escaped, some were killed in trying to escape, others killed in accidents, others died of disease and some, about 30 a year, served out their time and were released.

Most of the convicts came from the eastern part of the state. At one time there were 16 women convicts assigned to the camps along the track. The gangs were broken down into 10 or 12 men led by a foreman, prison guard, and captains. Guards received $13 a month as opposed to $25 a month for those who worked the prisons.

The convicts were worked six days a week with Sunday off. Convict labor halted work at 4 p.m. each Saturday and spent Saturday night playing music, dancing and getting ready for the next week's work.

Work details consisted of tree gangs which cut down trees, the chopping gangs which chopped up the trees and the digging gangs working on the roadbed.

All of the prison labor was under control of the state with the convicts being leased to the contractors.

Little has been written about the use of convict labor in building the railroad because that is the way business was done in the 1870's and '80's. It was the natural order, folks said.

The most remarkable feat in building the railroad came at the Blue Ridge escarpment between the villages of Old Fort and Black Mountain.

The rise for three-and-one-half-miles between Old Fort and Swannanoa Gap is 891-feet. This meant the road was laid out to encompass 2,776 degrees or eight complete circles. In fact, the roadbed almost crossed itself in places. Six tunnels ranging from seven feet to 1,832-feet had to be hand dug.

Another first for the construction in the South was the use of nitroglycerine for blasting cuts and tunnels. Before that, black powder or the old-fashioned method of putting cold water on rock heated by wood fires was used.

Two other feats stand out: First, a 450-foot-long cut that became known as "Mud Cut" because each day after convicts had shoveled out the mud, dirt and rocks, the mud flowed back in the night and the job had to be done over again. It took weeks to stabilize Mud Cut. Second, the convicts dug the Swannanoa Tunnel from both the eastern and western ends, meeting in the middle. To their credit, the place where the separate digs met was precise.

To take mud, dirt and rock out of the western dig, a railroad steam engine had to be dragged by mules, oxen and convicts using block and tackle the three-and-a-half-miles up the mountain and put on tracks at the western end of the tunnel. This process reduced building time of the tunnel in half.

As the crow flies, the distance from Old Fort to Swannanoa Gap is the same mileage as the route engineers hauled the engine. The railroad took nine miles to go that distance with its roadbed because of the curves needed to make the grade possible for steam engines and trains.

In all, 11 miles of road was built at a staggering cost of $2 million.

The politicians in Raleigh who preached economy in state government were very unhappy while the people in the mountains were elated that they now had a way to get their farm products to market.

A new day was dawning in the mountains.

Now to build the extensions to Tennessee - the Murphy Branch (now The Great Smoky Mountains Railway) and the Paint Rock section.

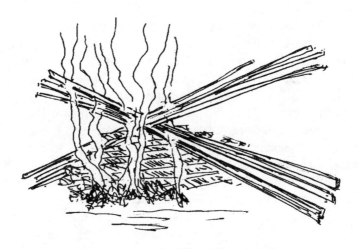

How Stoneman's Raiders Burned Rails

Chapter II

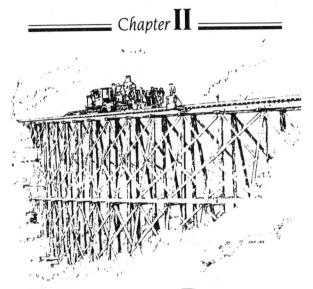

Building the Railroad

Construction of the "Murphy Branch" began in 1881 and was completed in 1894, many years after the target date for completion.

It, too, is a saga of mountain railroad building in the United States that, interestingly, is still ongoing.

The lore surrounding the 122.01 miles of the Murphy Branch includes the terrible deaths by drowning in the Tuckasegee River of 19 convict workers digging the Cowee Tunnel, thus giving rise to the story the tunnel is cursed; the remarkable rescue of a prison guard by a convict in the river drowning incident and the convict's subsequent beating with a leather strap by the prison camp foreman; train wrecks; wobbly track; floods; the struggle to get the roadbed over mountains and across rivers; a vendetta between the builder and a legislator, and more heroes than knaves.

It is also the story of the opening up of a frontier - the remote Great Smoky Mountains of North Carolina, a place called "The Back of Beyond" by author Horace Kephart when he lived in Bryson City after publication of his classic book on the mountain people, *Our Southern Highlanders*.

The Murphy Branch story began less than a year after the state-owned Western North Carolina Railroad completed the roadbed into Asheville from Salisbury.

The railroad's connections to Tennessee still had not been made, and the people of Western North Carolina were anxious to see the routes completed.

However, a problem arose: Newspapers in the eastern part of the state, as well as their politicians, didn't like the idea of completing the railroad. Gov. Zeb Vance of Asheville, a champion of the railroad in the mountains, had moved to the U.S. Senate and that move made Lt. Gov. Thomas J. Jarvis the governor. He decided the tax increase that would be needed for years to pay for future construction of the state-owned railroad was too high. The money, he said, should be used for education. Thus, he and the General Assembly cut a deal with William J. Best, a New York promoter, to purchase the railroad by paying the state $850,000 for its mortgage and pay $550,000 in first mortgage bonds plus other compensation to private stockholders.

The General Assembly, delighted to get out of the railroad business, approved the deal on March 27, 1880. One of the sweeteners to the deal was the railroad to Paint Rock and a junction with the East Tennessee & Georgia Railroad would be completed by July 1, 1881, and to Ducktown, Tn., and junction with the Marietta & North Georgia by January 1, 1885. Best also agreed to pay the state annual rent of $125 to the state treasurer for each convict used on the projects. Best needed the convict labor just as his counterparts building the route to Asheville had needed convict labor.

The only problem is Best didn't have any money of his own to purchase the railroad so he borrowed from three friends - William T. Clyde, Thomas M. Logan and Algernon Buford - to raise his share of the money. The three controlled the Richmond & West Point Terminal Railway & Warehouse Co. of Norfolk as well as the Richmond &

Danville. This loan would haunt Best in the future when he and a legislator picked a fight with each other over additional pay for convicts.

In the meantime, Best started construction.

Men and material were assigned to the Paint Rock connection that was to follow the French Broad River from Asheville to Paint Rock, just west of Hot Springs, a famous resort and spa because of its warm water springs.

Once Hot Springs became a station stop on the railroad, the hotel expanded by 100 rooms to accommodate more visitors than could reach the place via stagecoach.

Best's crews working from Asheville toward the Paint Rock connection followed the French Broad River, using sections of the old Buncombe Turnpike in some places for the railroad's roadbed, and in other places the new roadbed was blasted out of solid rock.

Part of the lore is how nitroglycerine was manufactured on the banks of Reems Creek in Buncombe County, stabilized with sawdust and cornmeal, and then transported to blasting sites each day in gallon jugs using a one-horse wagon and driver. The reason for the one-horse wagon and driver was containment of losses. If there was an accidental explosion enroute to the blasting site, the only loss would be the wagon, horse and driver. If the dynamite was manufactured at the site, an explosion could kill a number of people. No explosions are recorded.

In addition, Best also assigned survey and grading crews on the Murphy Branch line out of Asheville since he also faced a deadline for the track to Ducktown, Tn.

As the convicts and construction workers laid the track west out of Asheville, such station stops as Emma, Sulphur Springs, Acton, Hominy, Candler, Luthers and Turnpike sprang up. Some of the old place names still remain; only today they are hamlets and memories on highways 19-23, 74 and I-40.

Survey crews and woodcutters were clearing the right-of-way when William J. Best ran into a major problem that would cost him the railroad. A North Carolina legislator named Capt. Rufus Walker introduced a bill in the North Carolina General Assembly that required contractors hiring convict labor to pay an additional $1.50 per day to convicts in addition to the $125 per year.

Best was furious. It was an overhead cost that he had not built into his contract with the state when the state required completion of the railroad's branches by a certain date.

When he found out that the roadbed he was building would cut through a plantation owned by Walker at Valleytown, near the present town of Andrews, Best decided to spite the Western North Carolina legislator, grower and Confederate veteran. Best knew that by splitting Walker's land with the railroad he would be adding great value to the plantation. Walker could now build a town of stores and houses with his name on it and ship his farm products both east and west, so Best told his surveyors to bypass Walker's plantation and Valleytown and stake out a new route.

It would cost both men.

Best cut off Walker, but the change put the railroad behind schedule because a tunnel had to be built at Rhodo, three miles east of Andrews. The tunnel had to be reached by a steep grade, making track construction harder. Best was not a happy railroad promoter. He had gambled he could get to Paint Rock and Ducktown on time. Now he was against a deadline to reach Ducktown while at the same time construction costs were rising.

His creditors - Messers. Clyde, Logan and Buford - of the Richmond & West Point Terminal Railway, wanted some return on their investment - now! When they called Best's loan, he couldn't pay. So he assigned his interest to them, and they leased the Western North Carolina Railroad to the Richmond & Danville Railroad, a deal the North Carolina General Assembly turned down in 1875.

The Richmond & Danville sent Col. A.B. Andrews, its vice-president, to complete the line. Andrews, a civil engineer who fought for the Confederacy in the Civil War, is considered the man who conquered the Western North Carolina frontier. His legacy is not only a railroad but transportation in and out of the Great Smoky Mountains for the people who lived in the region, faster mail service and communication, fresh staples such as sugar, salt and flour as well as store bought clothing and tools, and the spawning of a new industry in the mountains - the logging and milling of lumber.

The chestnut, poplar and other woods of the virgin forest built the great cities of the East, and Andrews' railroad carried that lumber as well as the pulpwood that made the paper which American commerce found essential to do business.

When Col. Andrews undertook to complete the railroad's Murphy Branch to Ducktown, he also called it "temporary."

He was right to a degree, but as with many temporary things in this world, the railroad continues to maintain a permanent niche in the life of the mountains. Col. Andrews was no newcomer to railroading. He was considered one of the best railroad men in the South. He also was the nephew of Dr. William J. Hawkins, president of the Raleigh and Gaston Railroad and owner of other railroads in North Carolina. Andrews had worked on the various lines as an executive, while his uncle, Hawkins, was involved in Raleigh during the 1860's.

Andrews acquitted himself well in taking over the Western North Carolina Railroad. He brought in Frank Coxe of Philadelphia as vice-president; Vardry E. McBee as superintendent and Maj. James W. Wilson, one of the pre-Civil War contractors of the Western North Carolina Railroad, as chief civil engineer. Head of the survey crew was Col. Thad Coleman, same surveyor of the route from Old Fort to Ridgecrest.

Coxe is remembered best in Asheville as the builder of the Battery Park Hotel, a direct result of his working on the railroad and realizing that, with transportation into the mountains, visitors would be coming to view the magnificent scenery, and they would have to have some place to stay. Interestingly, his hotel, the first Battery Park, was built on the site of an actual artillery battery set up to defend Asheville in the Civil War, Battery Porter.

The new team under Andrews' command turned their attention to the completion of both connections, Paint Rock and the Murphy Branch.

In December 1881, the tracks reached Paint Rock where they joined the East Tennessee & Georgia with work being completed in 1882.

Col. Andrews and his men could now concentrate on the job at hand, reaching Ducktown, Tn., on time.

Twenty-two miles and a massive cut through a hill, the railroad reached the Ford of Pigeon, the actual ford where mountain people crossed the Pigeon River as it wends its way north toward Tennessee. Today Ford of Pigeon is called Canton, and how it was named is a story in itself.

The railroad called the station "Pigeon River" and then "Buford" after Algernon Buford, president of the railroad. Townspeople changed the name in 1894 to "Canton," the name it has been ever since.

Haywood County Historian W. Clark Medford, writing in one of his books, said one story has the town's businessmen meeting to select a name. They adjourned for lunch. When they came back one of the men on the committee looked up at the new iron bridge crossing the Pigeon River and noticed the lettering, "Canton Iron Works, Canton, Ohio." Since the lettering was already in place, he suggested Canton as the new name and it was approved.

As soon as the railroad reached the Pigeon River, a town grew up. While construction was being done on a railroad bridge across the river, Ford of Pigeon became a railhead. Shipments from afar consigned to Western North Carolina were off-loaded at the new hamlet. The shipments were loaded onto wagons for shipment to their destinations in the mountains west of the Pigeon River. Hogs, cattle and turkey flocks were driven to Pigeon River and the railhead for shipment to market.

Using pre-Civil War coaches, the railroad also carried passengers from Asheville to Pigeon River. One of the stories of passenger traffic on the 22-miles to Pigeon River is that the coaches were so hard riding that rubber was placed between the trucks and coach body to soften the ride over the wobbly track. When the railroad replaced the old shocks with new shocks, youngsters along the track took the old rubber shocks and turned the material into handmade baseballs for town teams.

There was a yearlong delay in moving the line westward from Canton, nee Pigeon River.

Lore has it Best held up at the ford while preparing to assign his interest to the owners of the Terminal Company. Actually, the delay was caused by the track crews' difficulty of getting through the wilderness west of Pigeon River. Flash floods beset the track layers as well as survey and grading crews trying to reach Waynesville and beyond.

It was a difficult job. Finally, in 1883 the railroad reached Clyde, a station stop named for William T. Clyde, one of the partners in the Terminal Company. Just as with Canton, Clyde turned into a railhead for a number of months as farmers and traders brought goods to the town for shipment to markets in North and South Carolina. In return, goods continued to move into the mountains.

When the railroad reached Waynesville in late 1883, the official celebration was scheduled for April 8, 1884.

Every town along the route had an "official" celebration with barbecue, speakers, bands and dancing.

The railroad, people knew, was going to bring Western North Carolina out of its isolation from the rest of the world, and the people wanted to celebrate that change.

Waynesville boomed after the railroad came. The Haywood White Sulphur Springs Hotel was built for tourists. In addition, several other hotels were constructed for "drummers," as traveling salesmen were known in those times, and business visitors. A knitting mill, Killian's, was built along with Coles Lumber Mill. The future looked bright. Prosperity was just around the corner.

Meanwhile, the grading and track crews led by Capt. A.E. Ward pressed westward toward Balsam Gap, the place where the Balsam Mountains had to be crossed at an altitude of 3,315 feet above sea level. In addition to construction, the track through the gap would give the railroad trouble throughout its history. One such story in lore has an excursion train stalling on the Balsam Mountain grade, and the passengers having to get off and push the rear coach to make sure the train got over the gap. In the mountains the Balsams are known as the "Plott Balsams," after the family which developed the Plott hound, one of the finest breeds around for bear hunting.

Tradition in the mountains says originally the railroad was to go through Webster, the county seat of Jackson County rather than down Scott's Creek and the Tuckasegee Valley. Lore and legend say supporters of the Scott's Creek route plied a state legislator with liquor so it would not go through Webster.

Webster was bypassed.

Closer to fact than lore is that survey crews originally considered boring 14 tunnels through the Balsams and the next range, the

Nantahalas, but instead decided to build a curving road through the gaps, taking much longer than anticipated.

Sylva, located on the Tuckasegee route, became the Jackson County seat. Its courthouse atop a hill at the end of Main Street is a photographer's dream as seen from the west lane of the Smoky Mountain Parkway (23-74).

The tracks reached Dillsboro, terminus of the present Great Smoky Mountains Railway just beyond Sylva, in 1883.

The next big obstacle in the way was a major bend in the Tuckasegee west of Dillsboro. The engineers decided to shortcut the bend with a tunnel through Cowee Mountain. This decision led to the greatest disaster in the building of the Murphy Branch, the death of 19 convicts working on the tunnel. Railroad publications also claim it as one of the horrible disasters in American railroad history.

(See Chapter III - Is the Cowee Tunnel Cursed?)

Nineteen convicts crossing the Tuckasegee River died when the flatboat guards were using to transport them overturned. In the lore of the mountains, problems with the Cowee Tunnel to this day stem from death on the Tuckasegee.

Once through the bore at Cowee Mountain, the rails followed the Tuckasegee River bank, crossing over to reach Whittier, site of an early Methodist Colony that later became a lumber mill town.

From Whittier the railroad followed more bends in the Tuckasegee into Bryson City, called Charleston before 1887.

Later it was named for Thaddeus D. Bryson, one of the prime movers in organizing Swain County.

Reaching Bryson meant another celebration, for now the major hurdle was crossing the Nantahala range that towered over the "Land of the Noonday Sun." Working out of Bryson City, the route followed the Tuckasegee River into a large valley, that would later become Fontana Lake, before swinging southwest toward the hamlets of Jarretts and Wesser and beginning the long climb through Nantahala Gorge to the hamlet of Nantahala and thence to a place called Topton in the gap of Red Marble Mountain. This route would give the civil engineers trouble before the roadbed would be finished. Col. Coleman's original survey held the grade to four percent while ascending Red Marble Mountain, but officials in the headquarters of the Richmond & Danville were unhappy about the steep grade and asked another opinion. The expert they called in walked the route, making hasty examinations of the land formation, and declared the survey by Coleman all wrong.

Richmond & Danville officials ordered a new survey from Nantahala to Topton. The new line was in some places only 50-feet below the old line, something the construction crews knew spelled trouble.

The reason, of course, is the easier route undercut the previous route laid out by Col. Coleman, and crews worried that each morning they would find landslides had closed the route they dug the day before. It happened as they had predicted, but they continued to dig on orders from their headquarters. The officials wanted an easier route.

The crisis came when a fellow named Will Sandlin Sr., whose son, Will Sandlin, Jr., later a legend in the mountains, headed crews digging a 500-foot tunnel through a part of Red Marble Mountain near the summit at Topton, and the expert hired by the Richmond & Danville made a test bore in the middle of the tunnel.

The bore gave the engineer bad news: Underlying the surface rock at Red Marble was white mud, the same type of white mud that had proved so troublesome at Mud Cut on the grade up Ridgecrest on the Old Fort Route into Asheville. On the Old Fort route the "jelly" like mud often boiled up overnight to raise tracks 20-feet by morning.

Col. Coleman apparently realized there was white mud under Red Marble when he drove his first stakes for the route, thus choosing a steeper grade, but one that could be completed without encountering the soft soil that makes road building in the mountains so difficult.

Nearly 90-years later engineers, working on I-40 through Pigeon River Gorge and on I-26 at Warrior Mountain above Tryon, would encounter mud slides that would delay and plague the builders for years.

So, for a third time construction crews returned to the bottom of the gorge and began building, this time following Col. Coleman's original survey route through the gorge. Instead of a tunnel at Topton, construction crews dug a deep cut of 43-feet at the crest of the mountain that is still in use today.

Murphy was still 28 miles and another major tunnel away as the crews worked their way through the gorge.

Not only did crews struggle with floods, cave-ins, mud slides and rock, but the severe mountain weather almost halted all construction at various times. Remember, the land between Asheville and Murphy was wilderness. Yes, there were a few towns and hamlets, but for the most part it was virgin territory served by trails and, maybe, a wagon road or two. The road through Nantahala Gorge was basically a widened footpath.

Winter in the Western North Carolina mountains is especially harsh since snowstorms hit with frequency. Rime ice often covers the higher elevations.

The winter of 1885 was one of those winters that residents back in the coves and along the ridges remember. However, for the men carving the railroad out of the wilderness, it was a winter never to be forgotten. Three feet of snow blanketed the Nantahala Mountains. Will Sandlin, the 19-year-old son of Will Sr., had a crew of 150 men camped above the roadbed they were building. There were two other crews at different locations that winter, all hampered by the heavy snow and ice.

Spring usually comes slowly in the mountains, climbing 100-feet a day up the mountainsides from the lower elevations. In the spring of 1885, there was a rapid thaw, as sometimes happens. With rapid thaws, water from the higher elevations cascades down streams and rivers, washing out trails, undermining footbridges, eroding embankments and tearing the ground away from level places.

The Nantahala River turned into a raging torrent that spring, tearing away embankments, track, the wagon road and trails down the gorge.

Will Sandlin's men rode out the storm and quick thaw, but they were cut off from supplies and knew it. There was no way fresh supplies could be brought from Bryson City over the washed out trails. The trails to Murphy went through wilderness. The best hope for the 150 men to eat was hunting small game. In fact, 48 hours after the flood, all food was gone except potatoes.

Under ordinary circumstances small game could be had, but the road building crew was made up in large part of convicts; many were murderers who would murder again to escape.

The convicts became restless when food supplies ran low. Guards kept their guns loaded at all times. It was a difficult situation. As time wore on and no supplies were forthcoming via the primitive path washed out from Red Marble Mountain to Bryson City, the men in the camp began to fall ill. Scurvy, based on a lack of Vitamin C in a diet, started, resulting in deaths. The situation was becoming desperate.

Sandlin decided to keep the men occupied, so he took ten of the worst criminals with him into the forest on a hunt for meat. The idea, he told interviewers later, was to keep the men occupied and the worst of then troublemakers out of the camp. The convicts got into the spirit of the hunt, and everytime one saw a squirrel, he'd shout and point it out to Sandlin. Sandlin would fire his rifle and the kitchen would have more meat. As the afternoon wore on, Sandlin noticed that the prisoners on the hunt would find more and more targets for Sandlin to shoot at. Sandlin thought about the possibility of running low on ammunition with all of the shooting he was doing to obtain food. If that happened, the chance of being jumped by the convicts was good. One-on-one he felt confident he could win. In telling the story years later, he admitted if the group had jumped him, he was a "goner."

Anything he did had to be natural.

He checked his ammo pouch and discovered he was down to his last shell. Just then one of the convicts pointed out another squirrel. Sandlin raised his rifle, took aim while hoping the squirrel would scamper away. The squirrel didn't move.

Finally, Sandlin lowered his rifle saying, "Reckon I've got enough for one day."

None of the convicts suspected that Sandlin was out of ammunition.

They formed up, and with the wild game at hand marched back to camp without incident. It was a close call, Sandlin noted, one he would not let happen again.

In the meantime, a fellow named Steve Whittaker who had a farm near Andrews on the west side of Red Marble Mountain, hitched up four oxen to a wagon and delivered 20 bushels of corn and other provisions to the camp. While the histories of the time do not note it, Whittaker apparently was provisioning crews from his farm as part of the commissary operation established by WNC Railroad employee D.S. Russell of Old Fort as the railroad moved up Nantahala Gorge.

Russell, according to R.W. Provost writing in the *Cherokee County History*, came to the county on specific orders of railroad officials to supply construction crews working west of Bryson City. Russell picked a place which is now in the heart of the Andrews business district, thus becoming the first resident of the town.

When Whittaker arrived, there was joy in the camp. Supplies still were weeks away at Bryson City, but nobody talked about what might have been had Whittaker not been able to make the trip. Before Whittaker arrived, a total of 19 men out of the 150 had died from scurvy. They were buried in flatland near Hawksnest trestle. Today the trestle is a fill.

Changes of the route through the gorge, along with the harsh winter and spring flood of 1885, ended all hopes the railroad would reach Ducktown on time. The delay on Red Marble Mountain cost the railroad two years and its goal. Traffic from the rich copper mines at Ducktown and Copperhill, Tn., would now flow in a different direction.

When the railroad failed to provide service by January 1, 1885, the Marietta & North Georgia rushed into Ducktown and also put track to Murphy and Knoxville.

Three obstacles remained: A trestle at Hawksnest, a deep cut at the gap at Topton and the tunnel at Rhodo. Sandlin, Jr., was given the task of building the trestle at Hawksnest.

Oxen teams and loggers went into the forest under the guidance of Sandlin to cut and trim some of the largest trees they could find. The trees were snaked to the site of the proposed 400-foot trestle. The trestle would be 43-feet high with sills 43-feet on the bottom deck. It would be a masterpiece of construction. The crews finished the trestle and it was precise. In later years some of the joints rotted out, and the railroad eventually replaced the trestle with a fill. But at the time Hawksnest trestle was a marvel of railroad engineering seldom seen in the United States.

With the track finally in place for the Rhodo tunnel, the rails were laid into Andrews, named for Col. A.B. Andrews, president of the railroad.

A small steam engine pulling a work train chugged into Murphy in June 1891, six years later. The Marietta & North Georgia was ahead and planning trackage toward Asheville when the financial panic of 1892 ended that road's dreams of eastward expansion.

While a first train had actually reached Murphy, there remained a great deal of work to be done. Abutments and culverts had to be built of stone. It was tiring and backbreaking work, but it had to be done to complete the road.

The only public event left for the Western North Carolina Railroad was the traditional barbecue dinner to celebrate reaching Murphy.

Cost of the route to Murphy had been too high. When a financial panic hit the country in 1892, the Richmond & Danville went into receivership.

It would be a new railroad from then on.

Crossin' the Tuckasegee River After Leaving the Cowee Tunnel.

Chapter III

Is the Cowee Tunnel Cursed?

Old-timers in the mountains say the Cowee railroad tunnel is cursed. Scientific people say it isn't.

The story of why some folks think the Cowee Tunnel is cursed is one of the interesting stories of railroading in the United States.

In trying to skirt a long bend in the Tuckasegee River, surveyors building the Western North Carolina Railroad decided to bore a tunnel through Cowee Mountain.

Remember, the same builders had bored a tunnel through Swannanoa Gap at Ridgecrest out of Old Fort on the route into Asheville. It cut off miles of grade. At the bend in the river just west of Dillsboro, the idea was to eliminate blasting the roadbed out of rock and at the same time putting down maybe several extra miles of track to accommodate the river's bend.

If you are going to blast rock, why not a straight line between two points?

The builders did. It worked.

However, in the process, says mountain folklore, the tunnel was cursed.

Folks who believe in the curse point to train wrecks in the tunnel, cave-ins, rock slides, sounds inside the tunnel, the dripping of water year in and out and constant problems involving railroading in the tunnel through the mountain.

It all began, they say, when 19 convicts died while trying to cross the rain-swollen Tuckasegee River on a Sunday morning in 1883 to begin a day's work.

The convicts, all Black men who were rented out by the state to do heavy labor on major construction projects, had gotten up from breakfast and gone down to the river from their stockade-style camp on the east side of the Tuckasegee.

Chained together with leg irons, the convicts were under the command of Guard Fleet Foster, a tough taskmaster. To move the men from the east bank to the west where the 836-foot tunnel was being bored, there was a ferry consisting of a flatboat hooked to a cable. By hauling on the cable, the boat would move across the river.

As so often happens in the mountains, heavy rains on the weekend had raised the river's level and turned it into a torrent. The guards, however, didn't seem to think the river any more dangerous than usual. There were a hundred or so convicts who had to be herded across the river to work on the tunnel. No time to waste. They boarded this group of 20 convicts, and Guard Foster ordered the boat shoved off.

A dozen or so feet from shore, the stern of the boat began to ship water. Immediately, some of the convicts became frightened and moved forward in the boat in an attempt to regain balance. The sudden shift put the bow under the water, and the flatboat capsized.

All 20 convicts and Guard Fleet Foster were thrown into the raging waters of the Tuckasegee. Despite being chained together, the convicts flailed about in an attempt to regain the east bank. The river was too swift and high, and the weight of the chains shackling their legs too heavy for the convicts to gain a handhold on the bank. They went under in a tangle of bodies and chains.

One convict, Anderson Drake, managed to reach the bank out of the tangle. Drake, a trusty, was not chained. When he turned around after reaching the east bank, he saw Guard Foster fighting a losing battle with the water. Drake plunged into the river and rescued Foster. When they both reached safety, there was no sign of the other convicts.

Amid the tragedy, Drake was hailed a hero.

Other convicts, and even the guards, figured Drake would be given a pardon for saving the life of a guard.

Foster lost his gun and wallet containing $30 in the rescue. He could understand losing the gun, but the wallet with the money was in a buttoned pocket. However, he had his life, thanks to the trusty Anderson Drake. Yet, the loss of the wallet bothered him. Wallets just don't pop out of buttoned shirt pockets.

When Drake and Foster returned to camp after the ordeal, Foster ordered a search made. Guards found Foster's wallet and the $30 in the wet clothing of Drake.

Instead of thanking Drake and recommending a pardon, the camp foreman ordered Drake beaten with a leather strap the maximum number allowed by state law - ten lashes. The punishment, so the story goes, was carried out in the camp yard in front of the other prisoners. Drake served 30 years, one year for each dollar stolen.

A few days after the incident, the bodies of the 19 other convicts were found. They were buried in unmarked graves on Cowee Mountain in sight of the tunnel they were building.

Drake, once a trusty, went back to work in the tunnel at hard labor.

Lore in the mountains says Drake put a curse on the tunnel, the camp foreman and Guard Fleet Foster.

John Parris, newspaperman, storyteller and author of a number of books on mountain history and folklore, says it is all mere speculation, hearsay, if you will, that's had a long way to travel.

In his version, one of many, he noted that the camp foreman was fired not long after the incident. Foster became ill and did not work again.

Great Smoky Mountains Railway President Malcolm MacNeil says, according to local stories, the year' round drips of water from the roof of the tunnel are the tears of the convicts buried above on the mountain. The sounds heard when in the tunnel are the moans and groans of the drowning convicts.

Once MacNeil and a dowser went to the top of the mountain to find the unmarked graves. The dowser, according to MacNeil, located the small cemetery and was actually able to pinpoint the graves.

"He made a believer out of me with that dowsing rod," MacNeil said. "And it is a scary place at night."

Engineers and firemen on the old steam engines aren't convinced the tunnel is cursed. They cite the fact steam engines release hot smoke and steam in rapid staccato bursts in the close quarters of tunnels and this has a tendency to loosen stone. They also cite the fact the tunnels were built very small and did not have concrete abutments, steel girders or anything to block falling rock.

Western North Carolina's brittle rock and the constant changes in temperature loosen the rock. This is a major problem today on Interstate 40 that travels through the Pigeon River Gorge. Rock slides are common on both the Tennessee and North Carolina sides, so much so that it seems as if one lane or the other is closed as crews clear rocks on an almost daily basis.

Southern Railway found out about tunnels in the steam age when its major tunnels in Kentucky on its Cincinnati, New Orleans & Texas Pacific subsidiary kept dropping rock (slate) and brick on engines and trains moving along the route. Those tunnels didn't have a curse on them. What the railroad found was steam locomotives huffing and chuffing through a tight tunnel loosened the slate and brick, causing them to fall. The CNO&TP engines had hoods placed on smokestacks in an attempt to halt the damage to the tunnels. It worked to a degree, but the hoods also pushed smoke and coal gases into the cab of engines, sometimes nearly overcoming engineers and firemen. This is why the route was known as the infamous "Rat Hole Division" of the railroad. As soon as a diesel-electric motive power replaced steam, the slate and brick stopped falling.

Construction and maintenance improvements have eliminated much of the danger today.

Yet, the story of the Cowee Tunnel remains part of the folklore surrounding the building of the Western North Carolina Railroad.

And there are those who don't think the "haints" have gone away. The Cowee Tunnel, they say, is still haunted.

The tears never stop.

Swinging Bridge

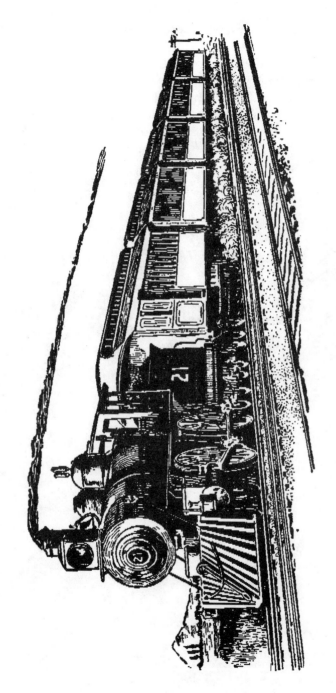

Chapter IV

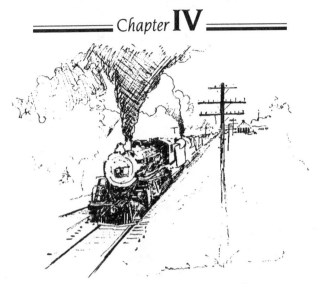

Southern's "Murphy Branch"

The year 1891 was not a good one for railroads in the United States despite the fact it was the beginning of the "Golden '90's," when tycoons reaped huge rewards for being part of the capitalistic system. That same system had some roller coaster rides for the very men it made wealthy. In fact, it made some of the wealthy quite poor. Or, as one wag put it, some men made small fortunes out of large ones.

For the Richmond & West Point Terminal Railway & Warehouse Co., the year 1891 was the end of the line and the beginning of Southern Railway, the company that emerged from the financial wreckage of the depression of that year.

The story is classic in that eventually the running of a railroad ends up in the hands of the financial wizards of Wall Street. The Richmond & Danville and its parent, The Terminal Company, were no exception to this rule. In fact, before 1893 was over, a total of 74 American railroads with more than 27,000 miles of line went into receivership. It was a debacle unmatched in American history.

The Terminal Company, Richmond & Danville's parent, was overextended. Its partners, Messers. Clyde, Logan, Buford and others, the same fellows who had called the loan on William J. Best when he was in a financial bind, had 70 mortgages bearing high interest rates on various properties when their bankers began calling loans.

This came at a most inopportune time. The Terminal Company, second largest railroad company in the United States, controlled one-sixth of all the railroads in the South. Only the Atchison, Topeka & Santa Fe had more rail miles than The Terminal Company.

Terminal, doing an annual business of $42 million, controlled more assets than any other company in the Chesapeake Bay region in 1893.

When the bankers would not extend more credit, The Terminal Company's whole southern network of rails began to unravel.

Georgia's courts didn't help matters in 1892 either when one of them annulled the lease of the Central of Georgia, one of the key components of The Terminal Company. The disintegration of the system began to gain speed after that decision.

John H. Inman, president of The Terminal Company, tried to refinance the company, but the package favored stockholders and bondholders over the firms that held the paper. The plan was rejected. Rather than accept receivership, Inman resigned.

Three receivers - Samuel Spencer, F.W. Huidekoper and Reuben Foster - were appointed to run the Richmond & Danville, and the East Tennessee, Virginia & Georgia lines.

Spencer, the architect of the Southern Railway System, was an interesting character. He was the son of Lambert Spencer, a wealthy cotton merchant and plantation owner who settled near Columbus, Ga., at an early age and married the daughter of Isaac Mitchell, a pioneer in the region. Samuel was an only child, and one of privilege. He grew up on a plantation where a life of ease was the norm for sons of wealthy parents.

The novel *Gone With the Wind* detailed the life of the Southern gentry before the Civil War. Sam Spencer lived it. He entered Georgia Military Institute at 15 years of age in 1862; when 17 he enlisted in Nelson's Rangers, a troop of cavalry that campaigned throughout Alabama and Mississippi in armies under the command of Generals Nathan Bedford Forrest and John B. Hood. It was under Hood the troop fought in the Battle of Franklin, Tennessee, a defeat for the Confederacy. After the war Sam Spencer returned to enter the University of Georgia where he graduated at the head of his class.

Instead of going back to the plantation, young Spencer decided to try railroading. Samuel Spencer attracted attention of Wall Street financiers by his work with various railroads. After service in New York and the Midwest in the late 1880's, he was named president of the Baltimore & Ohio. This assignment was short-lived as he tried to put the B&O on a sound financial footing over the objections of political appointees to the board. He left after a year and joined Drexel, Morgan and Company in New York City as an advisor on their railroad investments, a job he would hold the rest of his life, in addition to the presidency of the Southern Railway System.

When The Terminal Company went into receivership, Spencer and two others were named the receivers. Drexel, Morgan and Company was asked to reorganize The Terminal Company. Drexel named a committee and their consultant was Sam Spencer. A plan was formulated. All of the men involved in financing railroads wanted Spencer, and, with his election as president of the line, the House of Morgan was firmly in charge of the Southern System.

What he accomplished was remarkable. Instead of 30 railroads and 30 boards of directors, Spencer consolidated the railroads into one operation with one board of directors. He then went out to capture the weak lines in the South and did. This plan brought criticism that Northern bankers on Wall Street, specifically J.P. Morgan, were gobbling up Southern interests. They were, but there wasn't any other way to bring order out of chaos since all of the smaller lines that Spencer purchased or took over were bankrupt or nearly bankrupt anyway.

One of those lines was the Western North Carolina Railroad, the line leased to the Richmond & Danville by The Terminal Company.

When the Richmond & Danville went into bankruptcy, the state, which owned the right-of-way, decided to sell it to the highest bidder. The Southern purchased the old line at the courthouse door.

No sooner had Southern taken over the R & D lease than North Carolina Gov. Daniel L. Russell created a major problem for Southern and Spencer by attacking the lease. He and many legislators were angry that Southern was using Norfolk, Va., rather than North Carolina ports for traffic. Finally the General Assembly rejected the governor's thesis and affirmed the lease. In addition, the courts affirmed the lease too. Southern had the WNC Railroad as well as its main line between Goldsboro and Charlotte intact, a key piece in the Southern System.

The Murphy Branch would go chugging into the future under Southern leadership with an ironic twist - the Murphy Branch would furnish the Southern its last president of the railroad, Harold F. Hall, the man who would merge Southern with the Norfolk & Western in the 1980's to create one of the largest and most efficient railroads in the United States. It also would be the retirement home of another Southern president, William Brosnan, who was given an estate at Almond on railroad property that once was a retreat for Southern executives on Fontana Lake.

Under the Richmond & Danville banner, the Murphy Branch had ancient wood-burning steam engines and rickety rolling equipment. The tracks heaved and swayed every time a train ran over them. Woodcutters had to keep piles of wood along the right-of-way in case an engine ran out of fuel before the next stop.

Flash floods are a problem in the mountains as "gully washer thunderstorms" hit somewhere almost every afternoon.

The (Asheville) *Daily Citizen* reported such a storm in its Monday evening, September 11, 1893, edition, just before Southern took over the line:

"Rains Cause Trouble...Slides and Washouts on the Railroad."

"The unusually heavy rains of Saturday night, Sunday and Sunday night have caused the railroad men no little trouble..."

"Chief Dispatcher Newell of the Richmond & Danville received a telegraph this afternoon stating that logs were floating down the ri (Tuckasegee) river against the bridge at Bushnell at such a rate as to cause fear for the safety of the structure. A special train and a force of workers went out to the scene this afternoon.

"The eastbound train on the main line was an hour late this afternoon.

"The French Broad is out of its banks and on a 'tear' generally."

The next day *The Daily Citizen* reported on problems on the "Main Line" but said, "The Murphy Branch is conducting itself during these floody times to the admiration of all. It used to be that any sort of rain along this branch deranged the passing of trains. Now, none of the lines are 'holding up' better than the once derided 'goose neck.'"

The "goose neck" tag was given the Murphy Branch since it often was "down" because of floods, landslides and derailments. At least the rest of the world knew the Murphy Branch existed.

Typical of the early days on The Murphy was February 1891, when a storm washed away the tunnel trestle and damaged the lower trestle at Scott's Creek. In January 1892, a mountain flood knocked out trestles for three weeks.

The *History of Jackson County* notes that the same month the county had its worst accident on the railroad.

It seems engineer Sam France was backing Engine 252 down Dark Ridge grade to pick up some cars when the brakes on the train failed. Engineer France tried to halt the rolling train by putting the engine in reverse. A cylinder blew and the engine picked up speed going down the grade. The train jumped the track at the next trestle beyond Dark Ridge and sailed 140-feet into the air to land on the opposite bank of the creek.

Engineer France, fireman Arthur and brakeman Rufe Hemphill were killed. Brakeman Dan Hunsucker was critically injured. The history noted that both brakemen on the train were Black. The train was one of the line's freights.

A passenger train in those days usually consisted of an engine, baggage car and coach. In early days one passenger train a day went from Asheville to Murphy with another train going in the opposite direction.

Southern decided to make Bryson City headquarters of the Murphy Branch when business began to increase after the turn of the century. It also began replacing some of the trestles with fills, including the famous Hawksnest trestle near the top of Nantahala Gorge, to accommodate heavier loads of timber and milled lumber.

While it upgraded the rolling stock, the Murphy still received the bottom of the list in the Southern table of organization and equipment. The Murphy Branch went from one train a day in the 1890's to four trains a day in the 1900's, according to an old timetable.

There was an early daily train out of Asheville, No. 17, that left at 7:30 a.m., and arrived in Murphy at 3:45 p.m. There were 18 station stops and 22 flag stops in the 122 miles of route. The afternoon train from Asheville was No. 19. It made the trip every day except Sunday. It left Asheville station at 3:20 p.m. and arrived in Murphy at 9:50 p.m.

Running in the opposite direction, Murphy to Asheville, were trains No. 18 and No. 20. Train No. 20 left Murphy at 7:30 a.m. and arrived in Asheville at 1:35 p.m., while train No. 18 left Murphy for Asheville at 11:50 a.m., and arrived at 8:00 p.m.

Trains No.17 west and No.20 east met at Dillsboro at 10:55 a.m. each day except Sunday. Trains No.19 and No. 18 met at Willets at 5:20 p.m. each day except Sunday. Willets was a regular station stop four miles west of Balsam, and Balsam Gap. Dillsboro, of course, was a regular station stop and is now the eastern terminus of The Great Smoky Mountains Railway.

Today, The Great Smoky Mountains Railway covers six of the old station stops with its excursion trains from Dillsboro to Bryson City. They are Dillsboro, Barkers Creek, Wilmot, Whittier, Governors Island and Bryson City. Three of the six were flag stops.

One time a visitor to Western North Carolina had to ride the train from Asheville to Murphy, and his description of the road was "two streaks of rust and a right-of-way."

Author and columnist John Parris of Sylva (*These Storied Mountains* and *Mountain Bred* and other books) once did a column for *The Asheville Citizen-Times* on the "outlander" from Chicago who reported to his hometown Chicago paper on his ride on the Asheville Cannonball.

Parris wrote the "outlander" noted "this line had all of the weaknesses to which neglected railroads are exposed. The ballast was thin, the grades heavy and the ties rotten."

The famed Cannonball didn't go over 15-miles an hour even with the wind at its back, hence the name. Falling off tracks at that speed didn't result in much damage to either train or passengers.

Those regulars who rode the trains didn't mind. It was their ticket in and out of the mountains. They'd rather ride a train than walk, ride a horse or buggy to Asheville.

Yet, troubles continued to plague the Murphy Branch even with Southern in charge.

W. Clark Medford, Haywood County's historian tells a story in his book, *Land O' The Sky*, about an excursion train that stalled on the tracks outside of Canton.

It happened during one of the political campaigns of William Jennings Bryan, who ran for the presidency twice on the Democratic ticket. Medford said it was 1896 when Bryan, famed orator of the "Cross of Gold" speech, was to address an audience in Asheville during a campaign swing through North Carolina. People who wanted to hear Bryan had Southern Railway send an excursion train west to carry them to Asheville and then return to Murphy.

When the happy crowd returned the engine stalled just east of the "Canton Hill." The conductor announced that some of the passengers would have to get off to lighten the load.

W.H. Frazier, one of the passengers, later told Medford, "Not only did we get off, but we got off and commenced to push the rear coach."

With the help of passengers, the train started up and made the grade. The passengers walked the short distance to the Canton station and then got back on for the rest of the trip.

"I was used to helping push teams out of mud holes in those days," Frazier said, "but that was the only time I helped push a train over a grade."

Even in the 1990's steam engines may stall on steep grades. Norfolk and Western's famous 611 stalled on Saluda Grade about a half-mile from the top while pulling a rail fan train up the grade.

The slippage occurred, according to the local lore, because some boys applied a pound of butter to the rails the night before. Four other trips were made up the grade with steam engines without incident, but rail executives still remember the time when 611 slipped on the grade.

Southern was aware of the problems on the Murphy. Letters and complaints were routed to the railroad's district office. People complained of "bad equipment," "poor roadway," and "crowded coaches." As noted, the Murphy Branch wasn't exactly the main line. Its equipment was the oldest.

In 1910 the railroad announced improvements to the roadbed, ballast and track. Southern started the work near Whittier, where earlier in the year a bad accident injured some passengers. Rotted cross ties were said to have caused the accident.

The Waynesville Courier reported that Southern had begun work at Whittier to put down better ties and heavier rails along the branch line. The roadbed, the newspaper said, was in better condition than ever before. Southern moved some Santa Fe and Pacific type engines to the line to aid the usual Consolidations (1-8-0) locomotives assigned to the line. The original Consolidations were a combination of several competitive designs in the late 1870's and 1880's in the search for a suitable freight-service locomotive that could spread the engine's weight while negotiating the light (40 to 60 pound) rail of the time.

Finally diesel-electrics kept the trains moving around the curves and up the grades. Year after year Southern made investments in the Murphy to bring it up to par with the main line.

One of the reasons is that the railroad to Murphy opened up Western North Carolina to a new industry - the logging and milling of lumber. Until the railroad came, sawyers and the little peckerwood mills in Western North Carolina could not get either logs out of the forest or lumber to market. The Murphy Branch changed all that - forever.

With rail service, the lumbermen of Maine, Upstate New York, Pennsylvania, West Virginia and Michigan moved into Western North Carolina enmasse. They poked their own little logging lines up the sides of the mountains, into coves and hollows, anywhere timber could be snaked out and loaded for travel to the mills.

The mills sawed millions of board feet a month and shipped via the Southern's Murphy Branch. From 1900 until 1930 the Murphy Branch was a boom rail line. The railroad may have missed the copper boom at the mines and smelters at Ducktown, Tn., with rail shipments of copper, but it made up for its loss of revenue with logs and milled lumber bound for the cities of the Northeast and the furniture industry in Hickory, High Point and Statesville, all on the main line out of Asheville.

In 1907 when Champion Paper and Fibre out of Canton, Ohio, built on the Pigeon River, it purchased the pulpwood unusable for milled lumber. It turned the spruce and other woods into paper. Eventually, Champion became Western North Carolina's largest employer with one of the largest paper mills in the world on the banks of the Pigeon. It opened up its own logging operations throughout various tracts in the mountains. And it once held a major chunk of timberland in the Great Smokies near the present Newfound Gap area. Even today, Champion's wood-chip trains from South Carolina and Georgia plantations number in the hundreds of cars daily as they labor up Saluda Grade, the steepest railroad grade in the eastern United States. Saluda Grade is ten miles below Hendersonville. The cars are moved onto the Murphy Branch at Asheville, and the train goes to Canton for unloading. The cars are then moved back to the plantations for reloading.

It has been this way for 90 years.

The Murphy also gained in importance as the tourist industry spread throughout the mountains. People came for what the hucksters called the "salubrious" climate.

The present Jarrett House in Dillsboro is a prime example. Another hotel that owes its existence to the railroad is the Balsam House at Balsam Gap. It is still in operation. People rented rooms, took in the sun and good air, hiked trails and partook of fine food. The climate relaxed the visitors. Every station stop had a hotel, and the larger towns had two or three hotels catering to visitors from the "outland."

Tourism continues to be a major industry today in the mountains of Western North Carolina.

If the railroad moved people into the mountains, it also moved them out. When the cotton mills of the northern states moved south around the turn of the century, many of the tenant farmers and those who sold timber rights to the lumber companies took part in a mass exodus from the mountains to the mills. The railroad provided the transportation. The lure was hard cash at the end of the day rather than "make do" in dirt-floor cabins tucked away in the coves and hollows. Farming also was a losing venture at the turn of the century because farms, usually on the side of a mountain, were worn out from primitive farming practices, the slash and burn technique of opening up more land. Many farmers who could not make it with "nubbin" corn and didn't work timber went to the mills. Even today many Greenville and Spartanburg residents in South Carolina have kinfolk ties to families who remained.

While merchants in the town and farmers on the bottomlands were better off than the people in the coves and along the ridges, Western North Carolina was poor, very poor. This condition lasted well into the 20th Century.

Clark Medford said the "one event, above all others, that helped break this isolation and usher in improved conditions in this county (Haywood) took place here in the early 1880's - the coming of the railroad."

Medford summed up what local people thought of the "two strips of rust and right-of-way" with a chuffing and puffing steam engine and a string of cars making its way westward from the big city of Asheville. The train became the key to future life in the mountains.

The Murphy Branch proved its worth for Southern in the great flood of 1916 in the mountains of Western North Carolina. This flood knocked out Southern's main lines into Asheville.

A hurricane out of the Gulf of Mexico on the night of July 5, 1916, slowly wended its way north and collided with another hurricane front that rapidly crossed the Carolina coast northeast of Charleston, S.C., on the morning of July 14, 1916. By the next day, the front was over the mountains. When the two hurricane fronts stalled over the mountains, the result was 22.22 inches of rain in 24 hours in two different places.

One place was Mitchell, Avery and Caldwell counties, some 50 miles northeast of Ashevlle.

The other was Henderson and Transylvania counties, located 20 miles south of Asheville. Runoff from soil already saturated from earlier rains cascaded down creeks and rivers, crashing and smashing everything in sight before spreading out over the French Broad River valley.

The surge roared into Asheville, overwhelming the factory district and Southern's yards. Steam engines and trains were caught in flood surge as crews literally abandoned ship.

The earlier rains had raised the French Broad River at Asheville to flood stage.

When 19-inches of rain fell in Transylvania and Henderson counties during the 24-hour period on July 15-16, the headwaters of the French Board River couldn't handle the water.

When residents of Asheville went to work at 8:00 a.m. on July 16, the official flood gauge at the river was at 13.5 feet, some 9.5 feet above flood stage. That level in itself means high water along the riverfront.

At 9:00 a.m., an hour later, the gauge showed 18.6 feet. When the crowds watching the river rise looked to see the 10 a.m. reading, the bridge where the gauge was mounted floated away.

The river crested that morning at 21-feet.

It was a disaster of the first magnitude.

The death toll would reach 80, a majority in flash floods on streams and creeks in Western North Carolina. Nineteen people were swept into the water from a Southern Railway bridge near Belmont, N.C. Most died.

Virtually all traffic was stopped on the Southern's tracks, north, south, east and west into Asheville. Passenger train No. 12 was halted at Marion; No. 21, at Connelly Springs; No. 9's two sections at Melrose; No. 10's two sections at Saluda; No. 4 and No. 8 at Hendersonville; No. 28 at Nocona, and No. 12 at Paint Rock.

A total of 77 track washouts between Salisbury and Ridgecrest prevented trains from the east reaching Asheville. The same pattern existed north and west to Knoxville and south to Spartanburg.

Western North Carolina was isolated from the rest of the country except for one branch rail line - the Murphy.

Southern's stepchild branch railroad did not suffer the damage as its other three lines in and out of Asheville.

Southern immediately rerouted emergency supplies and food from Atlanta via the Western & Atlantic road to Marietta and thence to Murphy via the Marietta & North Georgia and finally through Murphy to Asheville over the Murphy Branch. Dozens of trains a day were able to supply the needs of the region as well as start the recovery.

Among those supplies: 900 kegs of track spikes, 200 kegs of "boat" spikes, 400 kegs of nails and 6.3 million board feet of lumber. In addition, food came via the line. All of these goods were carried on 525 freight and flatcars into Asheville. One railroader said there was a freight train of supplies rolling past a given point on the railroad every 30 minutes for nine months.

The Asheville yards were a disaster. The tracks were under a foot of silt that had to be carted away before a train could even move. Engines caught in the flood on both tracks and roundhouse had to be cleaned and refurbished. One road engine in the yards to be reworked for the Graham County Railroad, a logging railroad, simply disappeared into the French Broad River and to this day its hulk has never been found.

It was one time the Murphy paid for itself and then some. There also was a cost: The rail on the Murphy was left in rough shape because of the number of trains that used the line during the 1916 flood recovery. Southern practically had to rebuild the line after its heavy use.

The Murphy Branch became a key bridge line in the 1940's when the United States government decided to build Fontana Dam to supply electricity to Alcoa Aluminum Company's plant at Alcoa, Tn., during the critical years of World War II.

The Tennessee Valley Authority (TVA) was designated the builder of the dam at a narrow place on the Little Tennessee River in Western North Carolina. TVA, which had brought electricity to Eastern Tennessee when other power companies could not supply lines or power to homes back in the coves and hollows in the 1930's, found it necessary to reroute the Murphy Branch of Southern Railway from Bryson City to Wesser so the railroad would not be under water when the huge hydroelectric dam was completed.

The railroad followed the Tuckasegee River out of Bryson City to a station stop called Bushnell. This place is also where the Little Tennessee and Tuckasegee rivers join. It is the Little Tennessee the rest of the way into Tennessee. When the lake filled, Bushnell was under 236-feet of water.

Bushnell also was a key junction with the Carolina, Tennessee & Southern railroad that went to Fontana. It served a number of logging railroads that climbed the slopes bordering the Little Tennessee River valley. Many of those lines ran into what is now known as the Great Smoky Mountains National Park.

Lines ran to Proctor and Bone Valley, Noland Creek, Forney and other station stops. This branch off the Murphy, owned by Southern, served a thousand families or so in addition to the lumber mills. When the decision was made to build the lake, all of the villages, sawmills and farms in the bottomlands were covered with 300-feet and more of water.

The north shore of Fontana Lake would become the southern border of the Great Smoky Mountains National Park. Years later the only reminder of the civilization that once existed along the Little Tennessee and into the coves and hollows of the Park would be a number of small cemeteries that now can only be reached by boat and trail. Even now the closing of the north shore of Fontana Lake is a controversial subject in the region.

The project to reroute the Southern's tracks at Bushnell was begun in September 1943, and completed in two months. While the new link would be 15-miles long, it cut off eight miles from the old roadbed of the Southern. Unfortunately, the shorter run was offset by the fact the steeper grade for the new link reduced tonnage that could be handled by 40 percent. Southern's new link climbed one percent grade for five-and-one-half miles before dipping down an equal distance to the old Almond station.

TVA then built Southern a bridge across the Little Tennessee River that is 791-feet long and stands 179-feet high on piers. This bridge is one of the great scenic views of the lake on the Nantahala River run to Murphy by The Great Smoky Mountains Railway.

The Wesser link to the bridge is five-and-one-half miles of new roadbed.

Southern carried materials, such as 14,000 boxcars of concrete, for the building of the Fontana Dam over the roadbed of the Carolina, Tennessee & Southern along the Little Tennessee. Once completed, this track was torn up, and the waters allowed to cover the towns, farms and railroad of yesteryear.

Station stops along the new roadbed were named in honor of Cherokee Indian heroes. One is Tsali, named for the Cherokee who was executed, along with his sons, by the U.S. Army during the removal of the Cherokee from the Great Smoky Mountain area in order to save those who had fled into the mountain fastness of the Nantahalas and Smokies rather than face deportation to the Oklahoma Territory. The railroad also honored Chikalili, a longtime Southern employee who worked on that section of the line, with a station stop name.

Southern Railway continued its stewardship of the Murphy until losses on the line became more than $1 million a year in 1986. In 1978 the Murphy Branch of the Southern carried 2,223 cars. Nine years later the number of cars dropped to 817 cars a year. After reviewing the situation, Southern filed for abandonment of the 67 miles of track from Dillsboro to Murphy on April 6, 1988.

The railroad was running only three trains a week to Murphy with only ten cars a year to its terminus at Murphy.

A spokesman for Southern at the time said there were only ten major customers on the track from Dillsboro to Murphy.

Southern planned to retain trackage from Asheville to Dillsboro. Champion Paper Co. at Canton is on this part of the railroad. It receives four trains a day of wood chips for its paper mill.

The announcement brought forth protests from businesses along the Dillsboro to Murphy trackage.

How local government, individuals, local shippers and the state stepped in to save the track and aid in the creation of The Great Smoky Mountains Railway is a story of cooperation.

(In September, 1996, Hickory Nut Gorge, including the villages of Gerton, Bat Cave, and Lake Lure, south of Asheville and east of Hendersonville, were hit by a slow moving storm that dumped ten inches of water on the mountainsides in about two hours. This storm did the same damage to the area as the 1916 flood, forcing people to run for their lives, tearing out roads, bridges, dumping homes, cottages and business firms into the Rocky Broad River during its rampage down the gorge. No rail lines were involved, but the storm emphasizes the fact that Western North Carolina mountains are prone to flash flooding from storms.)

Proctor School Before Lake Fontana.

Timetable

ASHEVILLE—MURPHY (Central Standard Time)

Time Table No. 5 — In effect March 14, 1947

WESTBOUND									EASTBOUND			
THIRD CLASS			FIRST CLASS	Capacity of Tracks in Cars		Miles from Asheville	Division Nos.	STATIONS	FIRST CLASS	SECOND CLASS		
87 Daily	71 Ex. Sun.	69 Ex. Sun.	17 Daily	Siding	Other				18 Daily	68 Ex. Sun.	66 Daily	70 Ex. Sun.
A.M.	A.M. 6 20	A.M. 6 15	A.M. 9 30	Yard		0.0	S 142	L.v. (WCT ASHEVILLE .N) A.r.	A.M. 9 45	P.M. 12 45	A.M.	P.M. 12 30
.....	6 26	6 20	9 35			1.8	S 142	MURPHY JUNCTION F	9 35	12 31	.....	12 01
.....	6 46	5 26	9 41	25	61	6.8	T 6	BOSWELL	9 30	12 26	.....	11 55
.....	6 53	5 35	9 48	52	6	7.3	T 9	X .... ENKA	9 24	12 16	.....	11 45
.....	6 59	5 38	9 52	15	11	8.8	T F	HOMINY ....D	9 21	12 11	.....	11 40
.....	7 10	5 49	10 02	45	15	13.4	T 15	COBURN	9 12	12 01	.....	11 30
.....	7 30	6 15	10 14	....	Yard	18.1	T	WYXW CANTON .. NC	9 02	11 45	.....	11 15
.....	7 40	6 25	10 22	21	24	22.5	T 26	CLYDE ....D	8 52	11 25	.....	10 55
.....	7 54	6 32	10 29	26	....	25.7	T 26	LAKE JUNALUSKA D	8 45	11 15	.....	10 45
.....	8 38	6 38	10 35	53	82	28.5	T 26	WAYNESVILLE D	8 38	11 05	.....	10 39
.....	9 00	6 41	10 50	22	04	30.5	T 30	HAZELWOOD .D	8 33	10 50	.....	10 15
.....	9 20	6 55	11 03	27	9	35.3	T 36	CLARK	8 20	10 26	.....	9 50
.....	9 25	7 00	11 06	36	10	36.3	T 36	WCT BALSAM D	8 18	10 20	.....	9 45
A.M.	A.M.	7 16	11 18	60	....	40.1	T 36	WILLITS	8 02	10 00	A.M.	A.M.
8 10	.....	7 55	11 26	....	106	45.0	T	WYX ADDIE ....D	7 55	9 45	7 00	.....
8 30	.....	8 05	11 40	....	100	47.9	T 47	X ....SYLVA ....D	7 45	9 35	6 15	.....
9 30	.....	8 10	11 45	31	34	49.5	T 50	DILLSBORO .D	7 36	9 30	6 05	.....
9 50	.....	8 31	12 05	....	36	55.7	T 50	WHITTIER D	7 15	9 10	5 45	.....
10 00	.....	8 36	12 10	2	56.1	T 56	ELA		7 11	9 05	5 41	.....
10 30	.....	8 50	12 20	45	Yard	64.3	T 64	WYX . BRYSON NC	7 03	8 50	5 30	.....
A.M.		9 10	12 32	....	29	70.8	T 71	BROOKS	6 52	8 30	A.M.	.....
.....	.....	9 20	12 42	50	....	73.2	T 76	McCLAIN	6 43	8 20	.....	.....
.....	.....	9 25	12 46	....	12	77.5	T 78	W. ALMOND ....D	6 39	8 15	.....	.....
.....	.....	9 45	1 06	32	....	85.2	T 86	TALC MOUNTAIN	6 22	7 55	.....	.....
.....	.....	10 00	1 10	45	35	87.3	T 87	XWCNANTAHALA .D	6 18	7 30	.....	.....
.....	.....	10 25	1 25	18	28	91.4	T 91	TOPTON ....D	6 02	7 10	.....	.....
.....	.....	10 45	1 35	....	18	95.1	T 95	W. RHODO	5 53	6 40	.....	.....
.....	.....	11 20	1 50	Yard	100	100.2	T 100	X .. ANDREWS ....D	5 42	6 20	.....	.....
.....	.....	11 35	2 01	7	109	105.0	T 106	MARBLE ....D	6 32	6 53	.....	.....
.....	.....	11 50	2 09	29	109	108.3	T 110	TOMOTLA	5 25	6 45	.....	.....
A.M.	A.M.	12 15 P.M.	2 30 P.M.	73	119.3	T	118	YX .. MURPHY ....D L.v.	5 15 A.M.	6 20 A.M.	A.M.	A.M.
Daily 87	Ex. Sun. 71	Ex. Sun. 69	Daily 17						Daily 18	Ex. Sun. 68	Daily 66	Ex. Sun. 70

58

Chapter V

The Great Smoky Mountains Railway

Sixty-seven miles of Southern's "Murphy Branch" became The Great Smoky Mountains Railway in 1988 after citizens, shippers, local town and county governments, the state, Norfolk Southern Railway and "white knight investors" managed to agree on a financial deal to save the line.

The deal made the track and right-of-way state owned again with a lease to operate a railroad to a group composed of local shippers, private investors and a Florida insurance man who wanted to own a railroad.

The return of North Carolina government to the railroad business as track and right-of-way owner enabled private enterprise to save the railroad from its demise west of Dillsboro. A bit of government aid, combined with a bit of private investment, made sure factories and business firms along the line didn't lose the ability to ship goods by rail. And economically depressed counties in Western North Carolina have the opportunity to prosper because 184,401 visitors a year are riding the railroad's excursion service.

That, by any standard, is a pretty good deal.

Col. A.B. Andrews once said the line west of Asheville was "temporary" and it almost was.

Traffic on Southern's branch began its decline in the 1930's for several reasons. First, roads and highways between towns in Western North Carolina were improved to the point the railroad was becoming redundant. It wasn't the only mode of transportation. Second, the increased use of the automobile by mountain residents who now could get out of the hollows and coves by faster transportation than walking, oxen or horseback whetted their appetite for trips where the trains didn't go. Third, the decline of logging in the mountains by the early 1930's ended much of the reason for the railroad. With the trees gone, the market for milled lumber dried up. The only work in the woods was pulpwood cutting. Fourth, the small loggers began to haul pulpwood to Sylva's Mead mill and Canton's Champion Paper mill by truck rather than its being sent by train. This lack of traffic hurt Southern.

The building of TVA's giant dam at Fontana and World War II halted the decline temporarily in the early 1940's, but the die was cast in 1945 with the end of World War II and with the production of autos and other consumer goods for a public eager to buy.

In 1948 Southern ended its passenger service on the Murphy Branch. Not enough passengers were riding between Murphy and Asheville and intermediate stops. The Carolina, Tennessee & Southern ended operations with the completion of Fontana Dam in 1944. The customers of the railroad from Fontana to Bushnell Junction with the Southern moved to other places when their towns and hamlets were purchased either by TVA for lake bottom or, in the case of Proctor, Bone Valley, Hazel Creek, Noland and other coves, by the federal government as The Great Smoky Mountains National Park was extended to the north shore of Fontana Lake.

An era was coming to an end.

Freight car movements to business firms located along the line, while in decline, were still profitable enough for the Southern to continue operating the Murphy Branch.

Champion Paper Company at Canton continued to get its four trains of wood chips a day from plantations in South Carolina and Georgia. Mead Paper Co., later Jackson Paper Co., in Sylva, continued its production and shipments. The marble quarry at Marble, beyond Andrews, shipped, as did other firms.

Then in 1978 shipments again began a major decline from 1,627 carloads that year to only 770 carloads in 1987.

There was another factor. On June l, 1982, the Southern Railway System merged with the Norfolk & Western Railway to create one of the largest and most profitable railroads in the country - Norfolk Southern.

Ironically, the man who is credited with bringing about the merger as his greatest achievement as president of Southern Railway System, Harold F. Hall, was born at Nantahala into a railroad family.

His father, Odell C. Hall, was station agent in Bryson City; his grandfather helped build the railroad from Bryson City to Murphy; his three uncles all worked for Southern before they retired as station agents or section foremen, and Hall himself began his career with Southern as a teenage telegrapher at Wesser right out of high school while waiting for induction into the Navy, where during World War II he served as a gunner on a dive bomber in the Pacific Theatre of Operations.

(See Chapter VI - Three Key Railroaders)

Cut costs, generate business, increase efficiency and increase profits were the goals that a whole string of Southern presidents, including Hall, set many years before.

Despite Hall's ties to the Murphy Branch and his people in the mountains, Norfolk Southern could no longer sustain the losses despite trackage with a historical and glorious past.

The merger presided over by the mountain man, Hall, created a rail network of 18,000 miles, employing 41,000 people and grossing in excess of $3 billion a year.

As Burke Davis, author of the official Southern Railway history, *The Southern Railway - Road of the Innovators*, put it so well: "Hall emphasized that he would press vigorously for cost reductions."

A total of 67 miles of the Murphy would be abandoned, thus saving $1 million a year. The cost of running the branch from Dillsboro to Murphy through Nantahala Gorge was too much.

It was as simple as that.

So Norfolk Southern petitioned the Interstate Commerce Commission in 1986 for abandonment of 67 miles of the branch. There was an immediate, unhappy reaction among the people in the communities along the line that faced demise of their freight trains.

Officials from the towns and counties affected by the abandonment of service began trying to figure out how they could save the line and its service. Private discussions of how the rail line could be saved began with the Southwestern North Carolina Planning and Economic Development Commission whose members are public officials in the region. Various county economic development commissions and the chambers of commerce along the line also began looking for a way to save the railroad.

The private discussions among governmental officials, led by Dr. David E. Henson, mayor of the Town of Franklin and also chairman of the Southwestern Commission, continued until it was noted that, after a number of meetings, the options were slim.

Basically, the cost of the 67-miles of line would be too much for a company to take over and then attempt to recover its investment and make a profit for shareholders. Even at the rock-bottom price offered by Norfolk Southern, it would be a tough go.

Officials of the regional commission thought at one point they had a white knight in the form of a dinner train proposal by an Iowa firm that was successfully operating a dinner train in the Midwest. That proposal fell through when the firm could not obtain financing for a dinner train on the Murphy Branch.

In the meantime, Norfolk Southern continued the process toward abandonment with the Interstate Commerce Commission.

The price for the trackage quoted shippers and civic boosters before the abandonment notice was the estimated $650,000 salvage value. Norfolk Southern said if abandonment was carried out, the new price to any railroad would be $1.7 million, closer to the real value of the trackage.

An interesting thing happened on the way to the forum where community leaders, shippers and the public were going to discuss a last ditch attempt to save the line. Norfolk Southern sent a message that if the communities and shippers along the line would not fight the abandonment notice in hearings before the ICC, Norfolk Southern would keep open its offer to sell the track and right-of-way for the $650,000, a real bargain as far as railroad track goes.

It was a tense time. It would only take one shipper to upset the proverbial apple cart and file a protest.

Bill Gibson, director of the Southwestern North Carolina Planning and Economic Commission, consulted with his board, other planners along the line, civic leaders and shippers. The consensus was to tell Norfolk Southern there would be no challenge to the abandonment notice. In turn, Norfolk Southern agreed to delay as long as it could the abandonment in order to let the shippers and counties served by the track time to figure out a way to save the line.

The gentlemen's agreement held, but the counties, towns and shippers still could not come up with a solution to the problem, and Norfolk Southern was running out of time and money with its losses.

Both the Norfolk Southern and the Southwestern Planning Commission went separately to the state agency in the North Carolina Department of Transportation that leases other state-owned track to railroads to keep freight trains rolling in an effort to see what could be done. Unfortunately, there wasn't $650,000 in the Department of Transportation's budget for the purchase of trackage, and the General Assembly wouldn't be in session for a while.

In the past when track has been abandoned with no hope of further rail transportation at that time, the state would purchase the right-of-way for its "Rails-to-Trails" program whereby the right-of-way is turned into a hiking trail until such time in the future there again might be a need for a railroad.

Once lost, the cost of obtaining rights-of-way is prohibitive.

Mark Sullivan, director of the Department of Transportation's Rails Program, said the "Rails-to-Trails" program is really a plan of last resort.

He had been working with the economic development groups in the Southwestern Region for nearly a year-and-a-half before civic leaders decided to hold a public meeting to get ideas.

Even before the meeting he acknowledged two alternatives: l. A local group to save the line for the shippers and industry. 2. The trails idea.

"We're hanging in there to the bitter end," he said just before the public meeting.

The last ditch effort was co-sponsored by the Jackson, Swain, and Cherokee chambers of commerce, the Jackson County Committee of 100 and the Southwestern Commission.

Tom Massie, director of Jackson County's Planning and Economic Development, told *The Asheville Citizen* newspaper in an interview before the meeting, "We hope to determine a course of action."

Because of the scenic area in which the line travels, local officials hoped someone might take control of it and operate an excursion train as well as haul freight.

In the meantime, others had contacted Jim Bishop, director of Governor Jim Martin's western office in Asheville. He contacted Gov. Martin and the governor took an interest in saving the line. Sylva Atty. Orville Coward, a friend of Gov. Jim Martin, also contacted the governor about saving the line. The governor's office contacted Sullivan at the Department of Transportation and asked him to see what could be done. Money, it seems, was a problem.

The meeting was held in Bryson City at the Swain County Courthouse-Administrative Building on April 19, 1988. *The Asheville Citizen* called it a last ditch attempt to save the line. Something clearly had to be done.

It was an interesting meeting, not untypical in the mountains when community leaders are forced to face reality and cooperate when economic survival of their communities is at stake.

The meeting started out slow. Dr. Henson, mayor of Franklin and chairman of the Southwestern Regional Commission, moderated. All previous discussions were outlined. Failed options were reviewed and other options presented.

Then the first of the good news came.

Sullivan said Gov. Martin had contacted top officials of Norfolk Southern and was working with them to keep the line open.

Bob Scott, *The Asheville Citizen* reporter covering the Western counties, wrote in the morning edition the next day quoting Sullivan:

"Gov. Martin wants this line saved and this gives me a lot of confidence this will be done. Gov. Martin does not feel that abandonment is an option."

In his story, Scott noted Sullivan indicated the state might even buy the line.

Of course, right at that moment the state didn't have the money to buy the line. The state's purse strings were held by the Democratic majority in the General Assembly.

Gov. Martin's proposal also posed an interesting political incongruity. Here was a Republican governor advocating possible state purchase of railroad track and right-of-way when the conventional party wisdom nationwide was getting rid of state-owned railroads and allowing corporations to downsize as part of the survival of the fittest or "Economic Darwinism."

It also posed an interesting problem for Democrats. They are accused of taxing and spending. A Republican governor was planning to tax and spend to save a railroad that a major line said was inefficient. If there were to be purchase of the track, there had to be bipartisan cooperation to fund the purchase. The General Assembly had to give its approval, and the assembly was controlled by Democrats.

It was a bold move. And, of course, popular with the people in the mountains. It also was typical of North Carolina's governmental cooperation, both Democratic and Republican, with business in an effort to put the state into the nation's economic mainstream, an effort that began with the proposal to build a Western North Carolina Railroad in the first place.

Over the years, the focus of state government and private enterprise in the state had not changed.

Steve Stroud, president of the North Carolina Railroad, the state-owned company holding trackage and right-of-way in the state, said it was predicted that higher transportation costs in the next 10 to 20 years will make rail shipment of freight more attractive and that the state would try to keep the line open.

Scott quoted Stroud:

"People are going to be scrambling for rail service again. North Carolina intends to preserve the railroad."

He indicated the state was looking at bringing in a short line operator to operate the railroad if the rail bed is not abandoned.

State officials also indicated they wanted to purchase from Norfolk Southern the 22-mile stretch between Dillsboro and Waynesville in addition to the Dillsboro to Murphy track.

These proposals were dramatic for a public forum in the county courthouse-administrative building, but mountain meetings have a way of being dramatic.

Then Dr. Henson opened the meeting for discussion from the floor.

Atty. Orville Coward stood up and outlined his ideas and then introduced a Miami, Florida, insurance executive.

The executive, Malcolm MacNeill, chairman of the board of the Frank R. MacNeill & Son, a general insurance agency and two insurance-related companies as well as a director of the American Bankers Insurance Group and a lumber-holding company, said the railroad needed to be saved and he was willing, along with shippers being served by the line and investors, to purchase it from Norfolk Southern. He wanted to operate a passenger excursion line as well as a freight service to the shippers.

Joan MacNeill, later vice-president of the railroad, said: "We both have a long-standing interest in Western North Carolina and when we heard the railroad was being abandoned, we thought it too beautiful to be lost to the people of North Carolina."

The MacNeills have a permanent home in Western North Carolina.

The deal was put together in front of the audience with surprises that the local residents and planners had not heard about.

Of course, the shippers would go along. They needed the rail service. Advocates of economic development via tourism saw an unmatched opportunity for tourism. It worked just the way the advocates said it would.

The state would use its money and clout to deal with Norfolk Southern, which also leases other track important to the line.

And the "white knight investors," led by an insurance executive, would provide the operating capital and expertise.

In the business world it is what is called a "good fit."

With the meeting over, the tough negotiations began.

Gov. Martin had to get the Democratic majority on board the train, so to speak, or it wouldn't work. They had to pass legislation raising the $650,000 to purchase the track.

As noted before, mountain people pull together and cooperate when faced with the need to survive in a stoic pragmatism that overrides political philosophy, religion and differences in locale.

Liston Ramsey, the Democratic speaker of the House, represented three of the counties involved. He agreed with the concept and went to work to obtain passage of the funding.

Ramsey had his allies when he needed them. Democrats got the legislation rolling through committee and on the floor. Mountain legislators in the effort were State Rep. Jeff Enloe of Macon County, representing Macon, Clay and Cherokee counties; State Rep. Charles Beall of Haywood, representing Madison, Haywood, Jackson, Swain and Graham counties; House speaker Ramsey; State Sen. Royce "Bo" Thomas of Henderson County and State Sen. Charles Hipps of Haywood, both representing western counties in the Senate.

The General Assembly passed the enabling legislation in its annual short session with ease as a result of the powerful bipartisan support.

Now to buy the line.

State negotiations with Norfolk Southern were intense from April until July 19, 1988, when the contracts were signed.

Just days after the state purchased the line, a group of seven private investors and shippers along the line, led by MacNeill, signed a lease with the state for 25 years at $40,000 a year plus a percentage of its gross revenues.

Andrew Reichman, owner of Parker and Reichman poultry operations in Andrews, one of the largest shippers and a stockholder of the new railroad, said investors hoped to break even on the freight service and make a profit on excursion trains and a dinner train.

Gov. Martin announced the agreement between the state and Norfolk Southern to a cheering audience at a highway dedication in Cherokee on August 7, 1988.

The people in Western North Carolina were elated. It meant a brighter economic future.

Gov. Martin also praised Democratic legislators for joining with his administration in saving the line.

"The legislature was essential in saving this orphan railroad," he said at the dedication of the highway.

Much has been made over the fact the Norfolk Southern was within 48 hours of announcing it would pull up the track for salvage.

MacNeill and his investors installed Doug Ellis as president of the line with MacNeill as chairman of the board. Ellis, who served as president for five years, said getting the railroad started and operating was "a lot of work, but also a lot of fun."

"None of us knew anything about railroading so we did things differently. I think that was a plus. We were able to get up and running without following traditional methods."

Following Ellis' five-year stint as president, Malcolm MacNeill became president of the railroad with his wife, Joan G. MacNeill, vice-president and chief operating officer. She also is a bank director in Sylva.

The new owners set out to obtain rolling stock and engines.

Headquarters were set up in Dillsboro, the eastern terminus of the line, with a yard, shops and engine shed just west of Dillsboro.

Cars were purchased from a number of railroads and brought to Dillsboro where a GSMR crew refurbished them for use. Many of the cars retained their original road names and colors; others are painted livery colors of the new railway. The three club cars are from the Atlantic Coast Line and Seaboard. The Silver Meteor car ran from New York to Miami. The Dixie Flyer was on the Cincinnati to Tampa route, and The Champion operated between New York and Tampa.

The club and dining cars are operated on the dinner train in the evenings, the luxury or "varnish" train on the GSMR timetable. Dinner on the train is equal to those served on the best of trains during the heyday of American luxury travel in the 1920's when trains were extensions of the finest hotels in America.

Other cars were obtained from American Zephyr Railway, Northern Pacific Railroad, Seaboard Air Line Railway and Amtrak. The Great Smoky Mountains Railway also built open cars for railroad buffs who like to ride in the open. It is the open rear platform concept of "varnish" cars in the heyday of passenger railroading in the United States. The railway has between 30 and 40 cars available for its trains.

The railway has about 14 cabooses, many of them painted the colors of their original road along with logos and lettering.

GSMR President Malcolm MacNeill continues to search for cars to add to the road's roster of rolling stock.

Four diesel-electrics (GP's) and one Baldwin 2-8-0 Consolidations steam locomotive make up the power on the line.

The Baldwin has an interesting history. It was built in 1942 by Baldwin Locomotive Works for the U.S. Army. It was originally scheduled for use in Europe on the Army's military railroads. However, it remained in the states during World War II as an Army engine. It was declared surplus in 1946. A number of short lines used the engine on their roads until The Great Smoky Mountains Railway purchased the engine, No. 1702, in 1991 and put it into service on the excursion line in 1993.

The steam engine was in the motion picture, "*This Property Is Condemned,*" starring Robert Redford, Natalie Wood and Charles Bronson. Part of the lore of the railway is the train wreck staged on track just west of Dillsboro for another motion picture, "*The Fugitive.*" Wreckage of two buses and two locomotives from the Illinois Central may be seen as Dillsboro trains travel west toward Bryson City.

Diesel-electrics No. 777 and 711 were built in 1953 for the Union Pacific. Later they were acquired by the Chicago & North Western where they saw service before being purchased by the GSMR.

Engines No. 223 and 210 were built in 1964 for Norfolk & Western and saw service on that line before being purchased by GSMR.

The railway has 20 year-round and 75 to 100 seasonal employees.

The Great Smoky Mountains Railway maintains its 67-miles of track, as well as trestles and tunnels. Trackage between Andrews and Murphy has been abandoned because of a lack of freight loadings.

In recent years the railway has increased its number of investors with offerings of stock.

The railroad moved ahead in September 1996, when it was announced The Great Smoky Mountains Railway had purchased from the North Carolina Department of Transportation the 67-miles of roadbed of its line from Dillsboro to Andrews, trackage and right-of-way the state had purchased from Norfolk Southern to enable The Great Smoky Mountains Railway to get into business.

The railroad paid the state $625,000 for the tracks, as well as about $60,000 in 1996 rent and appraisal costs. Thus, the state got back its investment, along with rental.

The railroad agreed to allow access across its tracks to a new housing development in Swain County, and accepts, as part of the deed, a covenant that guarantees the tracks will be operated as a railroad perpetually.

Another one of its goals is to obtain the roadbed from Dillsboro to Waynesville. Negotiations for the 22-miles of track have been ongoing. Waynesville would like passenger service, as well as freight trains, in an effort to increase tourism to the city.

At one point Norfolk Southern indicated it was willing to sell to the state, and The Great Smoky Mountains Railway could lease the track as it has done from Sylva to Andrews for passenger service. However, in mid-1996 Norfolk Southern began a three-year $7 million improvement of the track and trestles on the 22-mile stretch from Waynesville to Sylva in order to haul long trains of propane gas for a new American Energy storage facility at Addie, east of Sylva.

Norfolk Southern also indicated it is not interested in running passenger trains on the same track as freights. The railroad is concerned with liability in passenger service.

MacNeill, an insurance man, said Norfolk Southern would require about $200 million in insurance if it permitted passenger trains to run on its Waynesville to Sylva trackage.

Liability is one of the reasons major railroads do not want to be in the passenger excursion business.

For rail fans and others, The Great Smoky Mountains Railway presents a good idea of what mountain railroading is all about. The railway has an average grade on its "level" places of 2.1 percent; while on Red Marble Mountain atop Nantahala Gorge, the grade is now 5.2 percent.

The railway has five regular excursions: The Tuckasegee River, Twilight Dinner Train, Nantahala Gorge, Red Marble Gap and Raft 'n' Rail. Some of these trains depart Dillsboro, some from Bryson City and some from Andrews. The line operates from April through December.

Has The Great Smoky Mountains Railway rescue helped the region?

If you talk with public officials, people involved in tourism and the economic-development people, the answer is yes. Based on the number of people riding the line per year, a total of 184,401 passengers in 1995, and national figures for spending by visitors, the line has generated an estimated $12 million a year in tourism dollars being spent throughout the Southwestern Region.

Dillsboro has revived with shops, restaurants and services along all of its streets. Bryson City's downtown is making a comeback after years of empty stores. The railway's potential for Andrews is still to be realized. However, business is on the upswing in the counties where the trains still roll.

State government and entrepreneurs joined to save a railroad and possibly a region.

The Murphy Branch is now The Great Smoky Mountains Railway, a new name in a long and proud history of mountain railroading.

(Rail fans might be interested to know GSMR diesel-electric engine No. 777, an EMD GP-7 built in 1953, carried number 274 when owned by Union Pacific and number 4282 when owned by Chicago & North Western. GSMR engine No. 711, also an EMD GP-7 built in 1953, carried number 239 when owned by Union Pacific and number 4400 when owned by Chicago & North Western. GSMR engines 223 and 210, both EMD GP-35's built in 1964, carry the same numbers with the GSMR as they did when owned by Norfolk & Western.)

Chapter VI

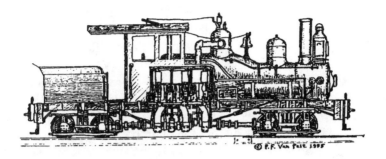

The Feeder Lines

If there were a commodity that kept the Murphy Branch busy from its completion in 1891 until the 1930's, it was timber. The great virgin forests of the Great Smokies made the line valuable beyond what the dreamers envisioned when they talked of a bridge railroad to the Midwest.

Logging in the Great Smokies and along the Balsams didn't hit its stride until around 1900 when timber barons from Maine, Pennsylvania, Michigan and Upstate New York discovered one tree alone in the Smokies could provide 18,000 board feet of lumber when sawed and dressed at a mill.

The mountain people who sold their timber rights to the timbermen never dreamed the timbermen could get out the logs. They knew that it often took a month to haul out five or six logs from one tree with oxen or horses. But they never figured on the

Shay steam locomotive, Climax engines, log loaders and overhead skidders.

They never figured on the narrow gauge timber railroads that the timber companies ran up the slopes of the Smokies and Balsams.

In less than 40 years it was all over. The timber boom had come and gone, and along with it, the feeder lines that kept the trains on Southern's Murphy Branch rolling.

One of the feeder lines, the Graham County Railroad, a timber railway for years, didn't give up the ghost until March 1975, when a storm knocked out two trestles and the railroad. It was a tourist line by then, and its owners decided not to rebuild the trestles. The Graham County Railroad, whose history goes back to 1905, originally was laid out to haul lumber for a number of companies cutting timber in the Snowbird Mountains, Santeetlah and West Buffalo creek areas.

Companies involved at one time were F.S. Whiting, Kanawha Hardwood Company, Champion Paper, Bemis Lumber Company and Gennett Lumber Company.

Its heyday was the 1920's to 1930's. Rails built into the mountains fed into the line's Bear Creek Junction and thence to Southern's junction at Topton.

Another line that fed lumber to the Murphy Branch was the W.M. Ritter Lumber Company which took over from Taylor & Crate on Hazel Creek in the Great Smokies.

Southern's branch line, the Carolina, Tennessee & Southern, ran from Bushnell, a junction with the Southern west of Bryson City where the Murphy Branch curved south toward Nantahala Gorge, to Fontana where in 1944 the Tennessee Valley Authority built a dam that created Lake Fontana.

Creation of the lake ended logging on Hazel Creek in the Smokies where the Ritter Lumber Company had timberlands. Ritter also had a village of Ritter on the railroad, as well as a town called Proctor in the Smokies, where logs were milled into lumber.

The Ritter line didn't have passenger trains as such but allowed residents of Proctor and other hamlets in the Smokies to ride the cabooses on the railroad's timber trains. Passengers then would transfer to the Carolina, Tennessee & Southern for the trip to Bushnell where they could travel west to Murphy or east to Asheville.

A timber firm called Babcock Lumber and Land Co. logged Slickrock Creek from 1917 to 1921, and its standard gauge railroad connected with Southern at the mouth of Slickrock Creek. The company used five Shay locomotives on its line. Often the logs were so large one log would take up an entire Southern flatcar.

Kitchen Lumber Company's logging line connected with Southern during the 1920's when it logged Twenty-Mile Creek, Barker Creek, Best Creek and Bear Creek areas.

Another logging line was operated by Whiting Manufacturing Co. in the present Fontana Village area. This line connected with Southern's branch running from Bushnell to Fontana.

The largest operation using logging lines connecting with Southern was Champion Paper and Fibre Co. Champion originally tried flumes to carry wood to its paper mill in Canton, but switched to rails from Sunburst, its logging village, to the Canton mill. Champion put rails nearly to Newfound Gap while logging the Smokies.

Its product, paper, was shipped via Southern. Today trainloads of pulpwood from South Carolina and Georgia tree farms make their way via Norfolk Southern to the mill at Canton.

The feeder lines made it possible to get logs to the mills directly in some cases and via Southern in other cases. Southern carried the finished lumber to market.

With the end of timbering and the coming of the Great Smoky Mountains National Park, freight car loadings on Southern's Murphy Branch dropped considerably.

With the development of bulldozers and logging trucks, the choice of loggers for transportation in the operations that were left, Southern had no choice but cut to back its number of trains on the branch line.

The Shay and Climax engines of yesteryear are in museums or chugging on excursion lines now. A Climax and log loader are exhibited at the Cradle of Forestry located in Pisgah National Forest near Brevard.

However, in the halcyon days of logging the feeder lines supplied the Murphy Branch with the bulk of its freight shipments outside the mountains. It was a grand era for the Branch while it lasted.

Backing Down From Topton.

Chapter VII

Railroaders' Memories

Gene Adams — Engineer

Gene Adams fired the last wood-burning steam engine used on the Western North Carolina Railroad. He also was the engineer on the first passenger train to Murphy.

In 1931 *The Asheville Citizen-Times* carried an interview story from Bryson City by Ann D. Bryson in which Adams, then a veteran of the railroad, talked about the early days on the Murphy line.

He told correspondent Bryson:

"Railroadin' in the good old days required men of brain and brawn and with cool heads and steady nerves, just as it does today, but they had to have more of these qualities to get by then."

Adams, who lived in Asheville in his later years, began as an apprentice boy in the shops of the railroad. He learned what he called the "why, wherefore, and when" of railroad machinery. It was a dirty job. He was covered with grease and dirt at the end of a day in the shops, but he also learned what railroading was all about. When he was 18-years-of-age, he was promoted to fireman. A few years later he was an engineer on a steam engine.

"I've seen many changes since I was old enough to remember in transportation and communications in Western North Carolina," he told correspondent Bryson. "Why, I saw the first telegraph wire stretched between Salisbury and Old Fort when I was a boy at home. My father lived four miles from Hickory and I remember one woman quarreled at the men for putting that line through her yard saying that every time she whipped one of her 'young 'uns' all the neighbors would know it. The road hadn't got to Asheville then. That was in 1876 or 1878."

He told about the early trains from Salisbury to Old Fort.

"When the first night train was run over this line, the section men walked the track ahead of it, leaving in time to cover their span and meet in the center."

Adams began as a fireman in 1885. In 1886, he fired the last wood burner on the Western North Carolina Railroad. When the interview was made in June 1931, Adams had been an engineer for 34 years.

"I was on one passenger run from Asheville to Murphy for 32 years and made that run on 29 successive Christmas days."

He also told Bryson:

"I've been using engine No. 902 for the past 12 years, the longest time I've ever used one engine. I ran the first complete passenger train to Murphy, the Smoky Mountain Special, on June 1, 1898, using an engine, one baggage and mail car combined, and one coach.

"This road first came to Pigeon River, now Canton, and the engineer had one helper, a fireman. W.B. Love ran this train. He would run out on a trestle, stop and then go back and collect the fares. A return trip was made each day. There was an engine, one coach and one boxcar. The first boxcar I ever saw looked as big to me as a warehouse does now. They handled no mail until the road was built to Waynesville, about a year later, and a conductor was added to the force.

"The next span was built to Calhoun, now Addie; then it was constructed to Charleston, now Bryson City, in 1888 and there was one train a day carrying passengers, mail and freight. The mail clerk was the late Bruce Freeman, the man who carried Senator Ransom off the battlefield when he was wounded while serving as a Confederate general. Sen. Ransom did a lot to get this road established."

Adams also talked about how much Bryson City had changed.

"The first time I came to Charleston (Bryson City), Dr. Scruggs was depot agent and had a boxcar down under a walnut tree for a depot. Manus Welch fed us and I've seen mountain trout on the table by the peck. It was dangerous to stick your head out of the cab window down by Nantahala, the trees were so close to the roadbed.

"Between here and Rhodo, I've seen gangs of wild turkeys, a few deer and once in a while a bear. From Balsam to Addie, I've stopped my train many a time and picked up a gallon of chestnuts, but we don't see any now."

The train, he noted, also stopped for hogs and cows that wandered on the track and refused to move for the iron horse.

"Why, our forefathers had a harder time getting a railroad into Western North Carolina than we have had getting the Great Smoky Mountains National Park. They did!"

Maj. Wilson of Morganton, a civil engineer who made his reputation building the railroad over the Blue Ridge Mountains; Robert Love of Waynesville; Felix Leatherwood of Webster; Col. Will Thomas of Jackson County; Hamp Hayes of Whittier; Col. Thaddeus Bryson of Bryson City, and Mr. Campbell of Murphy, with Gov. Zeb Vance, got it through. We should honor these men for there would not be any highways, any national park or anything much here, if they hadn't fought for a railroad. We shouldn't forget what these men did."

Charles Olson Hall
Station Agent

C.O. Hall of Marble was born, bred and raised a rail-roader in a railroad family.

His father, J.B. Hall, was a telegrapher and station agent who helped build Richmond & Danville's Murphy Branch in 1883.

J.B. Hall had four sons: J.E. Hall, a section foreman; O.C. Hall, an agent, telegraph operator and later a train dispatcher in Asheville; J.V. Hall, a station agent and telegraph operator, and C.O. Hall, the last station agent at Andrews after a long career with Southern Railway. The Hall family also produced a grandson, Harold F. Hall, who became the last president of Southern Railway and organized the merger of Southern with Norfolk & Western to form Norfolk Southern.

When old-timers talk of railroading on the Murphy Branch, the one name that always comes up is Hall.

C.O. Hall began his railroad career in 1924 on the "extra board" as did others hired by Southern. He was station agent, first at Wesser, then at Almond, the next station up the line, and then at Andrews.

"We were agents and telegraphers, but also handled all the freight too," he said in an interview for this book. "Remember, we had four passenger trains a day coming through, in addition to the freight trains."

Uncle C.O. went to Almond in 1943 so his nephew, Harold, who was awaiting call into the Navy during World War II, could work the Wesser station. Harold Hall's father, O.C. Hall, was station agent at Bryson City at the time. It was all in the family.

"I was single back in those days so I drove my car to where I worked. I went wherever they sent me. I liked working on the railroad."

Hall remembered one time he was working at Nantahala when one of the trains wrecked on Red Marble Mountain.

"That train just ran away on the mountain over there. It overturned 19 cars. The engine stayed on the track. It was just after he left Topton.

"And the passenger train, No. 17, wrecked up there at Rhodo. He'd (the engineer) left Topton and got down there almost to the (Rhodo) tunnel when he wrecked. The engine and baggage mail car went off. The wreck killed the engineer and fireman.

"Our shipments were mostly wood and lumber in those days," he added. "The trains would pick up lumber cars at sidings as they came along.

Passengers traveling from Murphy to Asheville paid $4.22 for a one-way ticket.

From Andrews to Murphy, a ticket was 34 cents."

Hall also spent ten years on the Winston-Salem Division, ending with 49 years on the railroad.

"In those days we didn't count the time," he laughed.

Hall remembered his nephew, Harold Hall.

"He'd come back and we'd see him. He was a good fellow. Always a good fellow."

"He was a railroad man," his uncle said. "He was a railroad man."

Coming from a railroader whose family literally built the Murphy Branch and worked it all their lives, it was the ultimate compliment.

James Fox — Engineer

James Fox received a medical discharge from the Army Signal Corps in 1943 because of asthma and joined Southern Railway as a fireman.

The Bryson City native retired as an engineer 18 years later in 1961, after having worked both in steam and diesel. He enjoyed every minute of it.

"When I started, the engines were hand fired. I was on 'extra board,' you went everywhere," he said. This put Fox in Winston-Salem, Greensboro, and even the Murphy Branch, part of the Asheville Division.

"We had a Winston-Salem Division engine crew. If you went toward Greensboro, then you were in the Danville Divison."

Fox finally came back to the Murphy Branch.

"After a good while, I stood for a job out here. I don't remember when that was, but it was on the last part of the steam engine days.

"The steam engines of that era were the '600 Class,'" he added.

"You know where they tore down the old Asheville freight depot and there is a little short street? Well, that's No. 722 and that's one of them."

The engine he referred to is now housed in a museum engine shed at the Asheville Chapter No. 153 of the National Railway Historical Society in Biltmore. It was loaned to the chapter by Norfolk Southern.

"That engine stayed at Andrews as helper over there. When I went to work those engines had 220-pounds of steam. They put bigger cylinders on them and cut the steam pressure down to 185-pounds."

Fox talked about taking engine No. 711 down the river (the Little Tennessee) when TVA was building Fontana Dam.

"Me and Joe Sawyer ran it from time to time when they were building that dam.

"It was on the No. 711 we took a hundred cars of cement. You could pull a hundred cars with one engine. Where the dam is at Fontana, they started at the bottom and built a flume. The river ran through it. Above the flume they had tracks. They cleaned all the building debris off the tracks each time we came and we put those cars in there. You could pull all those empties out of there with one engine."

One of the interesting aspects of the run down to Fontana from Bushnell is the engines went down backwards because there was no "wye" or "turntable" at Fontana. It was easier to back down the grade and then pull the cars out when they were empty.

"The cement came in boxcars. It was loose. They would suck cement out of those boxcars with a large vacuum system."

Joe Sawyer, the engineer, began his career in 1906. The old-timers taught the younger men.

Fox went to a packet of old books where all the rules of the road were outlined. He also pulled out seniority books so he could remember who worked the various engines and crews. The crews knew each other by the engines and trains they worked, but seldom saw each other face-to-face unless they were going out or coming in from a run.

Fox would pick out a name and say, "He came to work in 1888," or "this fellow was in 1890."

In those days they had Black firemen on the crews, and he noted they received less pay for doing the same job. Fox considered that unfair. Railroad crews, he implied, measured a man by what he could do and not by skin color.

Fox laughed when he talked about an engineer they called "Old man Hendricks."

"I'll tell you a good joke about old man Hendricks. Pat Colville was from Ireland. He came over and was firing for old man

Hendricks; we called him 'daddy.' He was a little bitty fellow who wore overalls that were clean and starched when he worked on those old 100's. Old man Hendricks was always working on his engine. One day he crawled up under there and got hung.

"He called for Pat and said, 'Pat, get me loose, I'm hung.'

"Pat said, 'Wait just a minute and I'll pull it (the steam engine) up off of you.'

"The fellow who told me about that, Leland Brown, said old man Hendricks came out from under that engine, and he was naked as a handsaw.

"He'd torn off his clothes to get loose."

Fox talked about filling the water tanks in the tenders.

"I remember old man Benjamin on a Charlotte job. We got water at Statesville, and we had to swing that thing (the water spout from the water tower) out and, as you filled the tender, you had to let it settle and then fill it up again.

"Southern said you filled it up, let it settle and then fill it up again. But the brakemen who rode out there in the doghouse (atop the caboose) didn't want you to let water run out on top of that tender because it would catch sparks; they'd dry up and then blow over on them.

"Benjamin said, 'By God, I always run it over and then we both know it is full.'"

Fox worked passenger trains, too.

"You worked all those jobs. You worked anywhere they called you for. Remember, you were on extra-board status.

"I believe I made the last passenger trip on the Murphy Branch in 1948."

Fox talked about the track in those days of steam.

"The (Southern) had good track back in the steam days. In fact, they had better track back in the steam days. They had it elevated. When they got diesels, they flattened it. It didn't have any elevation later."

His preference between steam and diesel?

"Diesel is a lot cleaner, but was more railroading with the old steam engine. Whistle blowing.

"Them old fellows could blow a whistle, some of them. They tuned that whistle. You know that?"

He went on to explain.

"Charles Saylor was a good whistle man. The steam whistles were round, and they had three cells in them - one long, one shorter and then a short cell.

"You had to screw it up and down to get the steam to hit it just like a little old whistle. When you found it, you'd mark it. Then make a copper washer and screw it right back down to that certain point. And if it didn't sound right, you put a dogwood block just about so big in the base; and, when you cut it off, it would woooo. He'd work on it. He made it sound pretty.

"You'd see people, well, down at Connelly Springs, three or four o'clock in the morning, people would turn on their lights and old Bull Moose would be a blowin' that whistle."

When diesels came in, Southern had some designers come up with an air horn that sounded like a steam whistle or, at least, as close as one could make it. That's why today Norfolk Southern's diesel air horns sound like steam whistles and still "woooo, woooo" in the night.

One of the infamous tunnels in railroading, the Cowee, just outside of Dillsboro toward Bryson City, was always an experience for Fox.

"When you were on a double-header, they'd put one engine behind and have one in front. That tunnel is little and crooked and hard to get right to the top, hard to get through there and you'd nearly burn up. It you slipped down, the engineer of the second engine in the double-header would hold you back in there until he'd see you weren't going to move. Then he'd let you back out and then we'd take another cut at it.

"Cowee was hard."

Fox said Balsam wasn't as hard.

"Balsam wasn't trouble. It was just a slow gait and you could keep up with it. But at Cowee you'd get hot. That's the trouble with my breathing now."

The hardest grade to go over, according to Fox, is Red Marble.

"Red Marble, I guess, is the hardest on this side. That railroad grade over there is the steepest east of the Rockies." (The Saluda grade on the Spartanburg to Asheville track is considered steepest with Red Marble a fraction less in grade.)

Jim Fox retired back home to Bryson City, where today The Great Smoky Mountains Railway keeps up the tradition of railroading in the mountains of Western North Carolina.

He misses the old times.

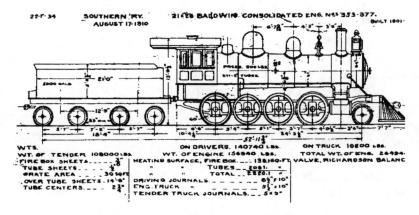

Baldwin Consolidated Engine 1901-02

Chapter VIII

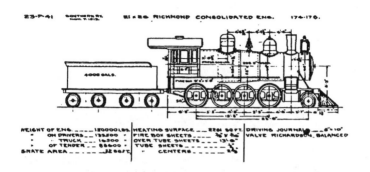

Three Outstanding Railroaders

Will Sandlin, Jr., Harold F. Hall and Bill Brosnan

Whenever the Murphy Branch is talked about, the names of three men involved with the mountain line always come up in conversation.

They are Will Sandlin, Jr., Harold F. Hall and Bill Brosnan. Sandlin and Hall were teenagers when they started with the railroad and made their first marks. Brosnan started after college.

Sandlin was a teenage construction gang foreman who built the road through Nantahala Gorge and beyond when the land was wilderness. He went on to become a legend in railroad and highway construction in Western North Carolina.

Hall was a teenage telegrapher and station agent, born and reared at Nantahala, who went to war and then came back to rise to the presidency of Southern Railway. He put together the merger of Southern and the Norfolk & Western into the present Norfolk Southern.

Bosnan, a rough and tumble man who grew up on a farm near Albany, Ga., and earned a degree in engineering at Georgia Tech before beginning his railroad career on a track crew, rose through operations to become the man, as president of the railroad, who changed Southern Railway's way of doing business.

All three men's lives are linked by Nantahala Gorge, Bryson City, Andrews and Asheville - the entire mountain rail line called The Murphy. All three are railroad legends.

Will Sandlin, Jr.

Author John Parris says Sandlin got his first job on the railroad mixing dynamite for construction gangs working on the Blue Ridge out of Old Fort when he was six-years-old.

Will Sandlin's granddaughter, Sara Posey Morgan, a resident of Andrews, doesn't say he was that young, but he was young.

The Sandlins were from Old Fort where Will, Sr., got a job on the Western North Carolina Railroad as a rodman on a survey crew in the 1870's when the railroad was climbing from Old Fort to Ridgecrest in a massive effort to cross the Blue Ridge and put tracks into Asheville. Will, Jr., and his brother lived about five miles east of a construction camp at Round Knob where their father worked, so they began to hang around the camp and watch operations as youngsters are inclined to do. They set up a brisk trade in chestnuts with the convicts assigned to the track construction crews housed at Round Knob. They gathered chestnuts to trade for tobacco.

Instead of blasting rock for the cuts along the line, the crews built fires next to the rock, heated the rock and then poured cold water on the rock, so it broke from expansion and contraction. It was a slow process, but one that was used because black powder was expensive. On the tough rock, black powder was used.

It was about this time the railroad hired an engineer who knew how to use Nobel's Blasting Oil, the invention of Alfred Nobel, the Swedish chemist who combined unstable nitroglycerine with sawdust to form a very stable product called dynamite. This new engineer knew the formula for dynamite, how to detonate it, and how to use it in blasting out rock cuts. The two Sandlin boys watched the mixing of the oil with sawdust with fascination. It all was really so simple that they begged to help. The engineer convinced their father mixing was harmless, so the boys mixed the stuff while hanging around the camp.

Sara Morgan says Will decided they could do better in the chestnut business if they mixed up a small lard tub of dynamite and put it under a giant chestnut tree they had discovered in the forest near camp. The idea was to shake the tree, and the chestnuts would fall out to be picked up and traded. Will and his brother placed the lard bucket full of sawdust and blasting oil under a major root and then laid a blasting cap. Will told his brother to get behind a big tree far away from the chestnut tree. He set fire to leaves and ran.

Will didn't make it behind the tree, according to family legend, and was buffeted by dirt and debris from the blast. His brother had to retrieve him.

Asked later what happened? Will's brother told the men, "I met Will when he was coming down and I was going up."

Will Sandlin, Sr., didn't think the incident funny; and, according to Parris, they made a trip to the woodshed in Old Fort.

You can't keep a good man down, so when he was 15-years of age, Will, Jr., left Old Fort by train to Asheville and Canton, then the end of the line, and walked all the way to Wesser, a 50-mile jaunt through the wilderness, to ask his father, then a grade foreman, for a job. He got it. At 18-years of age he headed a crew of 150 convicts building the rails up Nantahala Gorge to Topton.

This was in the spring of 1885; and a typical mountain freeze and thaw with hard rains had turned small streams into raging torrents, and the Nantahala River was over its banks, tearing out rocks, boulders, trails and even the roadbed of the railroad.

(See Chapter II for more details on this incident)

No supplies could get through to the camps; and Sandlin, to keep his men alive, had to hunt squirrel and rabbit in the mountains. One such hunt nearly cost him his life when he ran out of ammunition while guarding surly convicts and at the same time trying to hunt food to keep the crew from starvation.

One of Sandlin's triumphs is Hawksnest trestle, now a fill on the Nantahala track just before Topton. There was a deep gully on the road, and the question was to fill the deep gully or build a trestle? The chief engineer on the project decided to build a trestle and asked Sandlin if he could do it. The young builder looked over the blueprints and decided he could do the job.

Will Sandlin pondered the problem for some time before he took a crew and two oxen and went a mile down the gorge from Topton. The trestle was to be 400-feet long, 43-feet high, and have 43-foot bottom sills. He decided to have his men cut the trees, strip off the bark at the logging site, and then cut the various posts and beams in exact lengths for transport to the construction site. Once at the trestle site, each post and beam would be mortised and tenoned for joining. Sandlin was worried that all might not fit properly. He should not have worried as the whole structure went together perfectly.

Years later, the base rotted out and new joints were put together. Eventually the railroad decided to fill the gully around the trestle and today the Hawksnest trestle is a fill on the line. The decision to fill was made because of the constant shifting of the roadbed. When built, the roadbed had a four percent grade. It is now near five percent.

Sara Morgan tells about the time her grandfather brought his convict labor gang to Andrews for the celebration barbecue on the opening of the railroad.

"He was quite proud of those 150 convicts who built much of the line under his supervision," she said. "He wanted them at the barbecue; he brought them so they could have some good food after that period of starvation."

After a long speech, the townspeople, roughnecks from the hinterlands and the convicts were invited to partake of the food. The roughnecks pushed aside everybody and attacked the food on the tables as if they were starving. A major fight ensued with Will Sandlin, Jr., drawing a knife and slashing away at the roughnecks he considered an embarrassment to the townspeople and convicts who were being polite in lining up for food.

It was a hopeless battle. Sandlin backed off and took his convicts back to camp hungry after the free-for-all at the celebration.

Sara Morgan said her grandfather always declared that if he'd had his gun, he might have backed off the unruly crowd who ruined the party.

"My grandfather allowed his convicts shooting contests with both shotguns and pistols under his supervision while they were in camp. He purchased shot and shell out of his own pocket.

"He didn't want the convicts playing cards because too many fights broke out over winning and losing. However, if he kept them entertained with games of skill, such as shooting, there was less hostility and trouble within the camp."

Will Sandlin knew people and the men who worked for him.

Sandlin injured the forefinger on his left hand during construction of the Hawksnest trestle. Company doctors wanted to amputate the finger, but Sandlin said no. The finger did not heal properly, and ever after he was unable to use three fingers of his left hand.

Sara Morgan said the injury didn't seem to hamper her grandfather.

Will Sandlin suffered another injury, one that would take him away from the railroad and put him into a new career, the building of highways, roads and logging railroads in the mountains.

The injury to his leg came while building stone culverts and abutments along the right-of-way after completion of the track. Once the track was laid, crews went back to finish up culverts with stone work.

One day, west of Andrews, Sandlin's crew was working on a culvert. The idea was to use forged iron grabs and a windlass to hoist rock four-feet long and two-feet wide into place. The grabs were not working well, and twice during the morning Sandlin sent them back to the blacksmith for repair. Soon after the repair, a rock was hoisted into place. The grabs failed and the rock came down, crushing Sandlin's leg.

There was no doubt Sandlin's leg was broken so he ordered his men to cut some tree limbs to make a splint as well as two crutches. Because the crew was far away from the company doctor, Sandlin decided to tough it out. He took one day off and then hobbled back to the job which wouldn't be completed for a month. Then he went to see a doctor, but the leg had knitted poorly and Sandlin would limp the rest of his life.

When company doctors and lawyers discussed his injury, they told Sandlin if he wouldn't sue, the Richmond & Danville would give him a lifetime job. He accepted the offer. The Richmond & Danville went broke; and, when Southern picked up the line at the courthouse door in bankruptcy sale, there was no agreement to retain him.

His lifetime job had lasted two years.

However, Will Sandlin was too tough to let something like that get him down. He saw a new opportunity and took it. First, he took and passed a civil service exam given by the state for men with only practical experience for background. This examination allowed him to bid on state road construction projects.

At the same time, lumber companies were moving into Western North Carolina like armies on the march. Their task, as they saw it, was to strip every tree off the land, move the timber to sawmills and the lumber to market.

The Murphy Branch could move the timber to market and, in some cases, to mills. The problem was getting railroad tracks back into the hollows and coves so the huge logs from the virgin forests could be harvested and moved to the sawmills.

Will Sandlin, Jr., had built a railroad through the Nantahala Gorge to Andrews. This was ideal experience for building back in the hills, so Snowbird Lumber Company hired him to help with their 18-mile railroad out of Andrews into the Snowbird Mountains.

When he arrived at Snowbird Lumber, the company had six engineers surveying a route for the railroad. Sandlin decided to give the six engineers surveying the line a month to stake out a good roadbed. At the same time he took a look at how he would approach the problem. He also figured out what it was costing the Snowbird Lumber Company in overhead for the six engineers. He determined they were the company's major expense.

When no practical survey was ready at the end of the month, he fired the first two engineers. He waited another month and fired the next two.

One of the engineers was building a trestle near Andrews, so he went to see how it was coming. He found nothing fit and nothing was level. He asked for the engineer, only to be told the man was in Hendersonville, then a resort. Sandlin took the train to Hendersonville, where he confronted the engineer who told Sandlin, "I don't make mistakes."

"Then go take a look," Sandlin said. "I may be wrong, but it sure doesn't look right to me."

More mistakes on the engineer's part and he was gone. This left Sandlin with one engineer helper.

He told his assistant, "I'll build the road myself. I couldn't do worse than you fellows."

And build the road he did.

One of the many Sandlin stories involves his use of a transit in survey work for a 400-foot trestle over a gorge. The roadbed approached the gorge from both sides, and it was going to be Sandlin's job to line up the trestle's tracks with the tracks of the roadbed. He sweated this one out. Finally, early in the morning of the day work on the trestle was to begin, Sandlin hurried to the site before the workmen arrived and set up a surveyor's transit and lined up all the angles. He jotted down lengths of the poles needed, the beams and sills. When the workmen arrived, he gave the numbers to the timber cutters, telling them to fell the trees and cut the poles, beams and sills on the spot and then drag them to the construction site.

While Sandlin paced back and forth, the workmen erected the trestle. It was perfect. While Will Sandlin had never used a transit before in railroad and other road construction, he did after that, always lining up himself the various lines so there wouldn't be a mistake.

Soon he received calls from all over the region to build the logging railroads.

One he did for Champion Paper at Cold Spring Mountain turned out to be an incline railway that rose 3,500 feet in 4,200 feet. It was so steep that his men had to dig steps in the mountainside in order to stand straight.

Steel cables were 8,600-feet long, and it took a 65-horsepower loading machine and a 28-ton engine to haul the cables to the top of the mountain. Two tracks were laid. When cars loaded with pulpwood came down the incline railway, they hauled the 28-ton engine to the top. At the end of two years the mountain had been stripped and the incline came down.

Sandlin was working for the Andrews Lumber Company in 1913 when he received a call from the Graham County Lumber Company at Robbinsville. They wanted him to be "walking boss." He was assigned to build 10-miles of line from Robbinsville toward Topton where the Graham County line was to join Southern at a junction.

Construction of Sandlin's end of the line was going well, but the crews working on Red Marble Mountain were having a terrible time. The roadbed on the terraces built to hold track kept falling down. One day he rode over to where the crews were working to see the problem.

He noted that the terraces were too steep. He knew the foreman and told him that it wouldn't work. In fact, Sandlin noted a gorge nearby that would have put the Graham-Southern junction on level ground a bit down the Nantahala Gorge rather than right at Topton.

Sandlin mentioned this to his friend the foreman.

"I know, Will. I'm doing what the smart boys told me to do," the foreman told Sandlin.

A few days later the roadbed slid down into the Southern's track, causing not only delays on the branch, but an uproar in the Graham Lumber Company's office. The company had to hire a new engineer, clear the Southern tracks and start afresh on bringing the Graham County rails to the junction. The delay was costly.

Sandlin told them how to do it, but they continued to ignore him because he was an "uneducated mountain man who was earning more than they were and they were college trained civil engineers."

Sandlin's tracks on the sides of his mountains didn't fall down. He knew what he was doing.

Will Sandlin got into the highway construction business too. His most famous project is the Winding Stairs Road out of Nantahala Gorge to the top of a mountain in Macon County. The original path was a trail that in some places exceeded an eight percent grade. County commissioners decided to build a road and asked Sandlin to bid on it. He did.

Sandlin's gravel road is a masterpiece of highway construction in the mountains of Western North Carolina. It has never been duplicated and is in use even today.

Sandlin, perhaps, is far more well known for Winding Stairs than any other project.

Will Sandlin, Jr., passed away on March 27, 1947, in Asheville.

His granddaughter, a retired college professor and lawyer, continues to live in Andrews in the house where she was born.

Harold F. Hall — President of Southern Railway

Harold F. Hall was born at Nantahala where Winding Stairs begins. His grandfather, J.B. Hall, left Transylvania County near Brevard in the 1870's to work in the construction of the Richmond & Danville branch from Asheville to Murphy. He stayed for years as a railroad man, raising four sons, all of whom worked for the Southern.

His father, Odell C. Hall, was a station agent both at Bryson City and Andrews during his career with Southern. All of Harold's uncles were foremen or station agents all their lives.

Hall graduated from high school in Andrews in 1943 and decided to join the Navy. While waiting for orders to report, he learned Morse code from his father who was station agent at Bryson City at the time. The code came easily for the young man. The railroad needed a telegrapher at Wesser. His uncle, C.O. Hall, moved from Wesser to Almond, one station toward Bryson, so Harold could work the Wesser station. TVA was building Fontana Dam at the time, and Southern Railway was constructing track to bypass the future lake bottom. It was Hall's job to tell construction crews when trains were coming through so they could clean up debris along the track before a train arrived.

Hall worked in a little telegrapher's shack.

When he was president of Southern many years later, he loved to tell the story on himself when he determined to be a "hero" and save the railroad during a flood on the Nantahala River.

A rainstorm washed out some of the track at Wesser, and young Hall arrived on the scene not knowing who knew or didn't know about the washout.

He waded through knee-deep water to the telegrapher's shack, determined to do his duty and halt any trains due to come through.

As he told the story, he stood up to his knees in the water that covered the floor of the shack and opened the telegraph key.

Wham! The "juice" in the key blew him across the room and nearly electrocuted him. Stunned, Hall climbed up on the desktop, took out a pencil with a rubber eraser tip and then began to tap out the message that no trains could make it through Wesser because of the washout. Ever after, Hall was careful when standing in water.

The Navy called in 1944, and Hall became a crewman and gunner on a Navy dive bomber, seeing action in the Pacific.

As he tells it, the incident at Wesser was to be his last encounter with Southern Railway. He was going to receive his discharge in 1946, attend the University of Tennessee at Knoxville and receive a degree in electrical engineering. His railroading days were over, he thought. What really happened is, while waiting for college to begin, he got married and needed some money. Right at that exact moment an official of Southern needed a station agent telegrapher at Bryson City where his father had served. He was talked into a temporary job with the railroad. Promotions came very rapidly after that. Hall soon figured out he was never going to get to college, so he stayed with Southern, rising to become its president.

It was the railroad's classic "hometown boy makes good" story. He became Southern's expert on operations and transportation.

"I never considered myself a railroad man," he once said. "I was a problem solver. A problem solver in transportation."

Old-time railroad men who knew him dispute his view of himself, but the fact is his rise to the top job in Southern's executive suite was predicated on the fact he knew more about operations and transportation than anybody else in the company. He also came out of the Southern leadership program which concentrated on giving future leaders on the railroad the expertise usually reserved for graduates of the nation's finest management graduate school programs. When Harold Hall retired, he had a great college education and more, thanks to a positive attitude toward learning and doing.

One of Hall's triumphs was the safety program he installed at Southern, a program that paid handsome dividends in money and lives saved. Southern's "Green Light" program changed forever the way railroads ran. He also made it possible for freight trains to cross the country without being remade every time they entered the jurisdiction of a new railroad. He did that without official authorization and it worked.

However, his greatest triumph was putting together the merger of Southern Railway and Norfolk & Western to create the mega railroad Norfolk Southern.

The merger was the smoothest of any railroad in the nation, and it allowed two railroads to compete with the major railroads across the country.

Harold Hall was a mountain boy from out Nantahala way who made good in the big leagues of railroading and business after a start as a teenage telegrapher at Wesser. When Harold Hall died, Norfolk Southern asked permission of The Great Smoky Mountains Railway for his special funeral train to move along the GSMR tracks to Andrews.

The slow-moving funeral train with executives of Norfolk Southern made Harold Hall's final trip past Bryson City, where he was station agent in 1947; Wesser, where he began his career as a telegrapher; up Nantahala Gorge, where at the hamlet of Nantahala he was born, and over Topton to Andrews, where he was buried with honors, both military and civilian.

Harold Hall had come home to his beloved mountains.

Dennis William Brosnan — President of Southern Railway

There is an estate on the shore of Fontana Lake at Almond that once was a retreat for Southern Railway executives, the place they came to by rail from headquarters in Washington and the operating divisions to discuss and plan the future of the rail system.

It was a favorite of Bill Brosnan, a Georgia farm boy who saved enough money from hoeing cotton in the fields near Albany, Ga., to attend Georgia Tech and earn a degree in engineering, and many years later become president of the railroad.

The connection between Western North Carolina, the Murphy Branch, the estate at Almond and the president of the line is a story in itself.

The family had farmed the land around Albany for four generations, ever since the first Brosnan to America left Ireland one stop ahead of the sheriff. He had killed a deer illegally and for that offense, if found guilty, the British courts lopped off a thumb. The young Irishman preferred to keep his thumb, so he took a ship for America where he landed in 1810 and then worked his way down the coast to Georgia where he moved inland to Albany to begin farming.

Bill Brosnan's father, grandfather, great-grandfather, great-great-grandfather and great-great-great-grandfather all tilled the land until Bill came along. He wanted to be an engineer. He became one.

First with the Georgia Highway Department and then with Southern Railway.

Despite being ranked in the top ten percent of his graduating class at Tech, Southern put the farm boy on a track gang to start. It was here Brosnan encountered the rough and tumble ways at the bottom of the ladder on a railroad. The experience didn't bother Bill Brosnan. He had lived in bib overalls much of his life with only one "Sunday go to meeting suit," a suit that he passed down to his younger brother. Chopping cotton in Georgia fields taught Bill Brosnan about hard work. The lessons never left the kid from Albany.

Southern moved Brosnan from the track crew to its student apprentice program, the starting point for executives and many a Southern president.

From the school, Brosnan moved to Macon where for $50 a month he was an engineering assistant. He also courted and married Lou Geeslin, daughter of the chief clerk to Southern's Superintendent of Transportation.

When the Great Depression hit, Brosnan and his wife started a dairy farm to supplement their income. Brosnan milked the cows before going to work while Lou delivered the milk from a Model T Ford car.

He was to tell Burke Davis, author of *The Southern Railway - Road of the Innovators*, that the experience was "Christianizing" for him and his family.

He first came to the attention of Southern executives when assigned to check bridges and towers, and by climbing them, found damage to the structures. His report triggered repairs all along the railroad.

Brosnan moved up through the ranks - trainmaster, superintendent, and vice-president of operations. He really was an operations man, and out of this hands-on experience came the realization that Southern Railway had to change the way it did business or go out.

Safety became a key issue with him after he witnessed drunken railroad men killed in wrecks and under cars because they could not do their job. He determined to change that part of railroad culture and did. He instituted Southern's safety programs that gave the railroad the best record in the nation.

He also decided that the railroad needed to substitute mechanical power and effort for human effort. He had started out swinging a hammer and realized human power couldn't match the effort of machines in doing labor.

Brosnan ordered the design of many machines in track laying and other jobs to eliminate labor intensive work and ease the strain on railroad workers.

He also was a hard driving, tough boss who brooked no nonsense by anybody from the top down. He knew his job, and he also was determined to change the railroad's way of doing business.

He knew the rails, cross ties and every station along the routes of the various operating roads and divisions. He traveled 20 days a month in two office cars on the various roads and divisions. He also did not suffer fools or long-winded reports. *Fortune Magazine* said, "He is a hard driving boss; his subordinates often feel the sharp edge of his impatience at any carelessness, indifference, or imprecisions."

If he found any trains delayed, he wanted to know right away "why." The reason had to be good.

Brosnan figured out that the only way railroads were going to survive was to find better ways to haul goods in an unregulated shipping industry.

He took on the federal government's Interstate Commerce Commission, which set rail rates to aid other forms of transportation, and he won.

He ordered giant freight cars to haul wheat, coal and other products. He built huge automated marshaling yards in which to make up trains. He got into marketing, not his strong suit, by rehiring a former aide who once admitted he knew nothing about railroads, but knew marketing. The move worked.

Brosnan changed the way freight is hauled on railroads. This is his legacy.

He was honored by both *Modern Railroads* and *Modern Metals* magazines as Man of the Year in 1963. Sales and marketing executives across the country named Brosnan their National Salesman of the Year. This encompassed all industry. And in 1965 the Freedoms Foundation gave Brosnan its George Washington Medal of Honor for his effort in bringing about a better understanding of the American way of life.

When Bill Brosnan retired in 1967, the company he changed radically to keep it competitive in a new world of business, gave him the former Southern retreat at Almond on the Murphy Branch as a retirement home.

It was a gift the Southern could well afford, given Brosnan's record of profitability to shareholders and employees.

Today the estate is used by his family. His grandson is a doctor in Asheville.

Bill Brosnan learned to love the mountains of Western North Carolina while working on the railroad. He returned again and again both as the operating chief of the railroad and later in retirement until his death.

Today the estate at Almond is known as the Brosnan Place.

When people talk of railroading on The Murphy Branch, the names of Will Sandlin, Harold Hall and Bill Brosnan always come up.

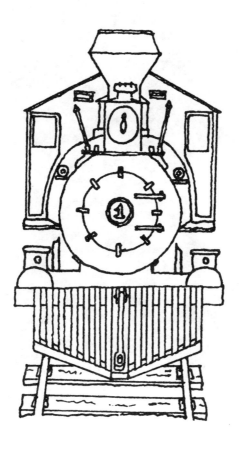

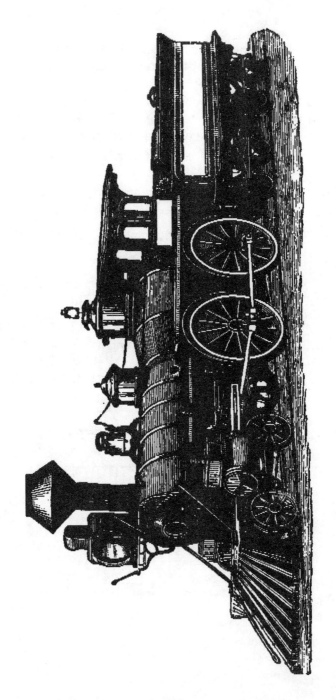

Chapter IX

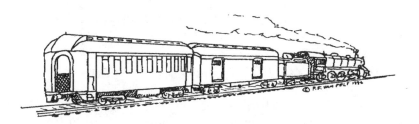

A Mountain Man Remembers

Nathan D. Greene grew up on a farm in the shadow of The Great Smokies, a half mile from the Noland station when his family's lifeline to the outside world was the railroad.

"It was the only way we could get anywhere," he said. "The state promised to build us a road, but they didn't do it."

Roads west of Bryson City toward Butner Branch, where his mother was born, Round Hill, Noland and Bushnell were simple sled paths or, in some cases, mere trails.

"This was a sled road. You could hardly get a wagon over it.

"You couldn't get to Bryson City, the major village east of Round Hill and Noland, without taking the train. Southern's tracks came out of Bryson City and followed the Tuckasegee River to Bushnell where the tracks then went south to Almond, Wesser and eventually up the Nantahala Gorge to Topton, Andrews and beyond.

"The station at Noland was approximately a half mile from our home place. My father would walk to Noland station to flag the train. It was the second station from Bryson City. First was Epps Springs, then Noland.

"One time, when I was a boy, they had four trains a day. I was just a young kid then. I remember one time we had to carry my mother over to the station at Noland, put her on a train for Sylva and the hospital where she was operated on for appendicitis. We couldn't get a doctor to come over the sled road. It was the only way to get to the nearest hospital. You took the train.

"They cut down to two trains a day, well, up in the 1920's. Then it went to one train. The meeting place was Bryson or Noland. You had to put the flag out, you know. It was ten cents from Noland into Bryson. And if you hurried up you could go into Bryson on that train, get your groceries, and then catch the next train back. Then to cross the Tuckasegee, we had a big swinging footbridge we walked over.

"If you came out of Proctor, you had to ride in the caboose. They didn't carry passenger cars on that railroad to Ritter."

Ritter Lumber Company operated the Smoky Mountain Railroad from its junction with the Carolina, Tennessee & Southern at Ritter to Proctor and Hazel Creek in the Great Smokies. This was one of the major logging railroads in the mountains.

"They'd have three or four flatcars of ore, too," Greene added. "They had freight trains, one a day. They'd go down and come back up."

The ore trains came from the Adams and Westfeldt copper mines in the Hazel Creek area and the Eagle Creek Copper Mine. The copper ore was shipped by rail via Bushnell, Andrews, Murphy and Ducktown, to the copper smelters at Copperhill, Tn.

"My father was a farmer and timberman. Timber was the only thing in here at the time, other than corn. Besides timber, our dependence was on corn."

Greene laughed about the corn and then said:

"We sold it by the gallon, mostly. I remember when a day's work was 25 cents or a bushel of corn. If you tended the bottoms (bottomland along the river), you could get help picking corn. We had a corn mill. My mother would grind. Sometimes for pay we'd give people a bushel of potatoes. People would carry the corn and potatoes three miles back up on Noland Creek where they lived.

"I didn't make very much corn liquor. I was too young. Me and another boy made some runs just to learn how. My father made some. Everybody did it. Mostly you drank your own or, maybe, sold some.

"Corn on these hillsides? You didn't grow anything but nubbins. We'd feed that to the cows. We didn't have any to sell until we took over the bottoms down there at Noland."

Greene helped his father harvest pulpwood and acid wood which the family shipped via the railroad.

"They shipped the pulpwood to Canton (Champion Paper and Fibre Co.) and the acid wood, the chestnut, went to Sylva and Andrews," he said.

"We made ties and cut telephone poles. It was mostly telephone poles at that time because there wasn't any electricity in the mountains.

"On timber, the railroad carried that all the time I was growing up. That's all the industry they had. Pulpwood and acid wood mostly.

"We used to cut acid wood for $5 a cord. We would peel jack pine for $5 a cord. And you had to peel every bit of it too. You know, when the sap's up. Trimmed into five-foot lengths and peeled.

"They called it a cubit because it was five-feet long. A cord was four feet by four-by-eight. Carolina Pulp Co. only bought it five-foot lengths."

Greene's father also worked for Ritter Lumber, located down the Little Tennessee River toward Fontana. In fact, he added, his father lost some fingers in a mill at Andrews, also on the rail line.

"He was tightening the saw and his hand slipped and went in between the saw. He also worked at Norwood Lumber at Forney's Creek."

In those days the timber workers stayed the week on the job and then returned home by railroad on the weekends.

"When TVA came in, it took the bottomland for the lake. Talahassee Power and Light Co., later Nantahala Light and Power Co., bought it all up along the river. They were not able to finance the dam. The government stepped in and TVA took over. Took all the land on the other side. Any land that went down to the water, they took the whole tract."

Closing of the railroad to Fontana via Ritter, the ending of timber cutting, building of Fontana Dam and lake, and the coming of the Great Smoky National Park resulted in an exodus of people from the Noland Creek area, as well as other towns along the railroad.

"As the people left, the grocery and general stores closed at Noland. We had to go to Bryson for supplies," he said. "Down at Noland there were two sidings. And the town had three stores. They brought the wood to these stores and they shipped it out. Folks hauled it to the store and bought groceries by trading the wood.

"About 1939 or 1940 they started changing the tracks. All the tracks were taken up along the Little Tennessee from Ritter to Bushnell after the Fontana Dam was finished."

Greene went into the Civilian Conservation Corps in 1937 and served two years at the Robbinsville Camp.

"The CCC is one of the best things this country ever did," he said. "We had 150 boys in there. We got along well, ate well and worked. I mean worked. Got a dollar a day.

"From seven o'clock in the morning until five o'clock in the evening, you worked for the U.S. Forest Service. From five until the next morning at seven, you were under the Army. They fed you, clothed you and sent $25 a month home while I was in camp."

The CCC saved many a mountain family since the $25 a month represented hard cash, something very few families living on subsistence farms got to see. Many mountain men today attribute their success in the Army during World War II and later to skills learned in the CCC.

"When World War II broke out, I began to work in steel," he said. "High buildings, dams, powerhouses."

Greene first went with TVA on some dam construction in Tennessee and Alabama. He then returned to work on Fontana Dam.

"I did ten or eleven jobs with them (TVA) in my lifetime."

He described how the railroad worked at the dam during construction:

"They shipped a lot of stuff in there during construction. Mostly cement. TVA had a big quarry down there, about 13 acres. All their crushed stone, sand, they made right there for the dam. All but the cement. The cement came in boxcars. They had vacuums and all that cement was vacuumed to a silo atop the mountain.

"The gravel was taken out of the quarry. It was hauled - nobody touched it - in big rigs. When loaded, it was shot down on yokes, the yokes took it to the back end of the hopper, the hopper crushed it, it then went across to the storage yard. They had a big feeder stair down in the ground. It would go down until it hit a conveyer. All the cement, sand and gravel would be conveyered all the way out to the top of the mountain. Each conveyer was about a hundred feet long and it would go one into the other. They claimed it was close to six miles. It went out to the top of that silo where it was mixed. There was a railroad under the silo that went out to the far end of the bridge. That railroad would go around carrying the 13 rigs that were pouring all the time, 24 hours a day. The rig would set down an empty bucket and pick up a full one and then swing it to pour, and then repeat the cycle. That train was going around and around day and night. Three buckets is all they could haul on each car; six-yard buckets on a 60-foot flatcar. Sometimes they were pouring 300-feet down. There would be a rigger with a cable air hoist. He would hook onto the bucket and pull it back under the bridge. It was air dumped. TVA had an air dump. They invented it. A man stood there with a high pressure hose. All he had to do was push it in and it would fit the cell," he said.

Greene was one of the 3,826 workers on the dam. Construction began in 1942 and was completed in 1944. The dam is 480-feet high and 376-feet wide at its base. It required 2.8 million cubic yards of concrete, all brought to the construction site on trains running from Bryson City. It also required 727,000 cubic yards of rock fill and earth. Cost of the project: $70.4 million. The lake covers 10,530 acres, is 30 miles long with a shoreline of 240 miles. The dam generates 283,000 kilowatts of electricity.

It took 15,000 acres of land from farmers and timber operators in the Little Tennessee Valley, wiped out a number of towns and villages along the river or in the Great Smokies.

With Fontana Dam built, Greene left the mountains for high steel jobs in Washington, D.C. He worked on all the major government buildings built after World War II. As with so many other mountain people who had to leave when jobs gave out, Greene came back in retirement to reclaim the two farms his family owned and grew up on.

Noland is gone. The lake covers the town. There is no swinging bridge. The rails are farther east. The road from Round Hill to Bryson is blacktopped.

But Nathan Greene remembers when.

Chapter X

The Western North Carolina Railroad — Epilogue

The Murphy opened the frontier of Western North Carolina. All of its owners continued the effort. Now The Great Smoky Mountains Railway opens another frontier - business and governmental cooperation in keeping open a key mode of transportation for business, while being the linchpin of tourism and other economic development in a region called "the back of beyond."

Loss of The Murphy would have set back attempts to develop the economies of the counties of the region. The western part of North Carolina has what other places do not have - awesome beauty. The problem throughout the years since lumbering died has been how to harness the beauty without destroying the very reason people visit the region. Many mountain areas have had great success, but at a terrible cost of urbanization.

The idea is to keep it the same and, at the same time, prosper.

The railway is the key. Expansion of its timetable, routes and rolling stock means that again the center of life along the route is the train.

State officials are correct: The train is making a comeback. The route is a valuable North Carolina asset. Gov. Martin did the right thing for the right reason. So did those in the General Assembly who supported the effort. The vision is paying off.

There will be a day when an interurban car, not unlike the famous Bamberger Car, will make its way along the main line. There will be a day when mail service may be more efficient in the region with a regular mail car. The potential is great.

The Murphy was built by people. The Great Smoky Mountains Railway is about people. It may be an excursion railroad, but it carries passengers. Few others can say that. The lessons learned anew by the GSMR in the movement of people may again be applied to other railroads as the transportation systems of the United States change.

Will Sandlin, Jr., Harold Hall and Bill Brosnan are gone, but their legacy lives on.

The road has a grand and glorious past and future.

Here comes the train! All aboard! The "temporary" railroad is still comin' 'round the mountain.

Acknowledgements

It takes a great many people, as well as institutions, to produce a book. Thus, I am indebted to many people whose help and effort deserve recognition.

These are: Alice Lawson, my editor on two book projects in the past three years. Without her counsel, editing and advice, this project could not have gone forward.

Gil Crouch, a book seller, who first suggested that I undertake writing a book about the Murphy Branch. This book is a result of his suggestion and encouragement.

Tom Massie, former director of the Year of the Mountains and former director of the Jackson County Economic Development and Planning Commission, and Bill Gibson, director of the Southwestern Economic Development Commission, for their interviews and information on the chapter concerning the efforts to save the railroad.

Philip Van Pelt for his illustrations included in the book, and his comments concerning the manuscript.

James Killian Spratt, well-known sculptor, artist and friend, for his illustrations on events contained in the book.

Joan MacNeill, vice-president of The Great Smoky Mountains Railway, for her cooperation in an interview and answers to questions submitted to her.

Lisa Roberts, assistant professor of Library Science and Head of Special Collections at the Ramsey Library at the University of North Carolina at Asheville, for her help in locating photographs and other information pertaining to the railroad.

Tim Daniels, Special Collections of Ramsey Library, for his help in locating photographs needed for illustrations.

Greg Frizzell, head of Special Collections at Western Carolina University's Library for his help and counsel.

Priscilla Proctor, assistant in Special Collections at Western Carolina University, for her help in locating material and photographs for illustrations.

Members of the Research Desk at the Western Carolina University Library, for their help in locating manuscripts pertaining to the railroad.

Sara Posey Morgan, granddaughter of Will Sandlin, Jr. for two interviews, a video, and location of key materials needed in chapters where her grandfather played a key role in the building of the railroad.

George Morgan, great-grandson of Will Sandlin Jr., for his help in securing interviews, videos and information.

Former railroaders C.O. Hall of Marble and J.E. Fox of Bryson City for their interviews on what it was like working on the railroad.

Nathan D. Greene of Round Hill for his interview on the railroad before and after the construction of Fontana Dam.

Doug Ellis, first president of The Great Smoky Mountains Railway, for his interview on getting the railroad up and running.

Juanita Barnett, Faith Printing Co., sales representative, whose suggestions were invaluable.

Deron Edwards for his cover design and counsel on the book design.

Tammy Owings and Teresa Howard for their production comments and counsel.

Others I would like to thank include Mimi Cecil, who served with Mrs. Morgan on the board of the N.C. School of the Arts, and suggested the interviews; Espie and James McClure Clarke, former congressman for the Western North Carolina district, who suggested interviews with people familiar with the railroad and its operation; Aileen R. Ezell, vice-president of Asheville Chapter No. 153, National Railroad Society, for information on the chapter's museum engine used by Southern Railways in Andrews as a helper; Karen Gibbs, who read the manuscript, for her suggestions; Charles "Buddy" Chapman for his work as a photographer in securing material for illustrations; Joyce Morgan Fogerty, assistant librarian at the Henderson County Library, for her help in locating materials; Jacque Beddingfield, an instructor at Blue Ridge Community College, for her suggestions concerning illustrators; the staff in special collections at Pack Library in Asheville; research assistants at the Wilmington, N.C. Public Library; staff at the Haywood County Public Library, Waynesville; assistant librarians at the Cherokee County Public Library in Andrews, and the Canton Historical Society for information on the railroad.

And especially, my wife, Diane Darden Parce, for her patience on many trips to locations during research and interviews involved in the writing of the book.

My sincere apologies to anyone I have carelessly omitted.

Sources

Interviews

Charles Olsen Hall, Marble, retired Southern Railways station agent.
Nathan D. Greene, Round Hill, resident for whom the railroad was a lifeline.
J.E. Fox, Bryson City, retired Southern Railway engineer.
Joan MacNeill, Dillsboro, vice-president, The Great Smoky Mountains Railway.
Doug Ellis, Waynesville, first president of The Great Smoky Mountains Railway.
Sara Posey Morgan, Andrews, granddaughter of Will Sandlin, Jr.
Tom Massie, Waynesville, former director of the N.C. Year of the Mountains and former director of the Jackson County Economic Development and Commission.
Bill Gibson, director of the Southwestern Economic Development Commission.
Channel 2 video interview with Malcolm MacNeill, president and chairman of the board of The Great Smoky Mountains Railway.

Bibliography

History of Railroads in Western North Carolina - Cary Franklin Poole.
The Asheville Citizen-Times - 1910-1997.
The Asheville Citizen - 1893-1894.
The Asheville Citizen - 1931 - Ann Bryson - Feature story.
The Western North Carolina Railroad - 1855-1894 - William Hutson Abrams, Jr. - Unpublished Thesis, Western Carolina University.
Southern Railway, Road of the Innovators - Burke Davis.
History of Jackson County.
History of Cherokee County.
History of Swain County.
Land O' Sky - History-Stories-Sketches - W. Clark Medford.
The Early History of Haywood County - W. Clark Medford.

Mountain People, Mountain Ties - W. Clark Medford.

Railroads in Western North Carolina - Spencer Bidwell Reiss - Unpublished Thesis, Western Carolina University.

Prince of the Carpetbaggers - Jonathan Daniels.

The Great Smoky Mountains Railway Souvenir Booklet.

All Aboard - Booklet - *The Great Smoky Mountains Railway.*

Channel 2 videos.

Southern Steam Power - Harold E. Ranks and Shelby F. Lowe.

Railroad Magazine - Article on the Murphy Branch - 1948.

Pack Library Research Files - Newspaper and magazine clippings pertaining to Railroads in Western North Carolina.

Mountain Bred - John Parris.

My Mountains, My People - John Parris.

Roaming the Mountains - John Parris.

Trains, Trestles & Tunnels - Railroads of the Southern Appalachians - Lou Harshaw.

Hazel Creek From Then Till Now - Duane Oliver.

Strangers in High Places - The Story of the Great Smoky Mountains - Michael Frome.

A Piece of the Smokies - A Pictorial History of Life in the Smoky Mountains - Ed Trout and Olin Watson.

Last Train to Elkmont - Vic Weals.

Cross Ties Over Saluda - John F. Gilbert and Grady Jefferys.

Birth of a National Park in The Great Smoky Mountains - Carlos C. Campbell.

The Great Forest - An Appalachian Story - Appalachian Consortium.

Our Southern Highlanders - Horace Kephart.

The Carolina Mountains - Margaret Morley.

Western North Carolina - Its Mountains and Its People - Ora Blackmun.

Western North Carolina Since the Civil War - Ina W. Van Noppen and John J. Van Noppen.

Miners, Mill Hands and Mountaineers - Ronald D. Eller.

Railroading - Boy Scouts of America Merit Badge Handbook.

Leahy's Hotel Guide and Railway Distance Maps - 1910.

Official Railway Guide.

The North Carolina Railroad, 1849-1879, and the Modernization of North Carolina - Allen Trelene.

North Carolina Board of Railroad Commissioners - Proceedings and Reports.

N.C. Department of Transportation Report, *Rail Corridor Acquisition Critical Needs.*

Index

A

Acton 25
Adams, Gene 77, 78
Adams & Westfeldt 104
Addie, N.C. 70, 79
Albany, Ga. 98
Alcoa Aluminum Co. 54
Alcoa, Tn. 54
Almond, N.C. 46, 80, 95, 97, 100, 104
American Energy Co. 70
American Zephyr R.R. 69
Amtrak 69
Andrews, Col. A.B. 25, 27, 35, 60
Andrews Lumber Co. 94
Andrews, N.C. 34, 69, 70, 71, 80, 82, 88, 91-97, 104
Arthur, --- 47
Asheville 1, 4, 11, 13-16, 24-37, 47-53, 60, 75-81, 88-95
Atchison, Topeka & Santa Fe R.R. 44
Atlantic Coast Line 68
Avery County 52

B

Babcock Lumber Co. 75
Biltmore, N.C. 82
Baldwin Locomotive Works 69
Balsam Gap 29, 48, 79, 85
Balsam House Hotel 51
Balsam Mountain 4, 29, 73
Baltimore & Ohio R.R. 45
Barker Creek 48, 75
Battery Park Hotel 27
Battery Porter 27
Beall, Rep. Charles 67
Bear Creek 75
Beaufort 11
Bemis Lumber Co. 74
Benjamin, ---- 84
Bennett, James 12
Best Creek 75
Best, William J. 24-26, 44
Bishop, Jim 64
Black Mountain 21
Bone Valley, N.C. 55, 60
Brevard, N.C. 75, 95
Bronson, Charles 69
Brosnan, D. William 46, 87, 88, 98-101, 110
Bryan, William Jennings 49
Bryson, Ann D. 77, 78
Bryson City, N.C. 30-32, 47, 54, 61, 64, 71-82, 85, 88, 95-108
Bryson, Thaddeus D. 79
Buford, Algernon 24, 25, 28, 44
Buncombe County 25
Bushnell, N.C. 54, 55, 75, 104
Butner Branch 103

C

Caldwell County 52
Caldwell, Dr. John 11
Calhoun, N.C. 79
Campbell, --- 79
Candler 25
Canton, N.C. 28, 51.60, 61, 75, 78, 89, 105
Canton Iron Works, Ohio 28
Cawtaba River 16
Carolina Pulp Co. 105
Carolina, Tennessee & Southern R.R. 55, 60, 74, 75, 104
Central of Georgia R.R. 44
Chicago & North Western R.R. 69
Champion Paper and Fibre Co. 51, 60, 61, 74, 75, 93, 105
Charleston, S.C. 12, 17, 52
Charlotte, N.C. 14, 15, 46
Cherokee County 64
Chikalili, 56
Christiansburg, Va. 16
Cincinnati, Ohio 68
Cincinnati, New Orleans & Texas Pacific R.R. 40
Civilian Conservation Corps (CCC) 106
Civil War 15.19
Clyde, N.C. 29
Clyde, William T. 24, 25, 28, 29, 44
Cold Spring Mountain 93
Coleman, Col. Thad 20, 27, 31, 32
Coles Lumber Mill 29
Colville, Pat 83, 84
Connelly Springs, N.C. 53, 85
Copperhill, Tn. 34, 104
Coward, Orville 64, 66
Cowee Mountain 30, 37
Cowee Tunnel 23, 37, 40, 85
Coxe, Frank 27
Cradle of Forestry 75
Crouch, Gil 2

D

Davis, Burke 61, 99
Davis, Jefferson 15
Dillsboro, N.C. 30, 37, 48, 51, 59, 62-68, 70, 71, 85

Dix, Dorothea 14
Douglas, Sen. Stephen 14
Drake, Anderson 39
Drexel, Morgan & Co. 45
Ducktown, Tn. 12, 24, 25, 27, 34, 104

E

Eagle Creek Mine 104
East Tennessee & Georgia R.R. 24, 27, 44
Ellis, Doug 68
Emma 25
Enloe, Rep. Jeff 67

F

Fisk, Jim 19
Flat Rock 15
Fontana Dam 54, 83, 95, 106, 108
Fontana Village 75, 105, 106
Fontana Lake 30, 46, 55, 60, 74, 98, 100
Ford of Pigeon 27
Forney, N.C. 55, 105
Forrest, Gen. Nathan Bedford 45
Foster, Fleet 38
Foster, Reuben 44
Fox, James 82-86
Frazier, W.H. 49
France, Sam, 47
Franklin, N.C. 62
Franklin, Tn., Battle of 45
Freeman, Bruce 79
French Broad River 12, 25

G

Geeslin, Lou 99
Gennett Lumber Co. 74
Georgia Military Institute 44
Georgia Tech 88, 98
Georgia, University of 45
Gettysburg, Pa., 17
Gibson, Bill 63
Goldsboro 14, 46
Gould, Jay 19
Governor's Island 48
Graham County R.R. 54, 74
Graham Lumber Co. 94
Grand Rapids, Mich. 17
Graves, State Sen. Calvin 14
Great Smoky Mountains 1, 4, 73
Great Smoky Mountains National Park 55, 60, 75, 79, 106
Great Smoky Mountains Railway 1, 3, 13, 30, 40, 48, 55-59, 69-71, 85, 96, 109
Greene, Nathan D. 103-108
Greensboro, N.C. 82
Greenville, S.C. 521

H

Hall, Charles Olson 80, 95
Hall, Harold F. 46, 61, 80, 87, 95-97, 101, 110
Hall, J.B. 80, 95
Hall, J.E. 80
Hall, Odell C. 61, 80, 95
Hall, J.V. 80
Hayne, Robert Y. 12
Haw River 17
Hawkins, Dr. William J. 27
Hawksnest Trestle 34, 47, 90, 91
Hayes, Hamp 79
Hayward White Sulphur Springs Hotel 29
Hazel Creek 60, 74, 104
Hemphill, Rufe 47
Henderson County 12, 15, 52, 53
Hendersonville, N.C. 51, 53, 93
Henson, Dr. David E. 62, 64, 66
Hendricks, "Daddy" 83, 84
Hickory, N.C. 51
High Point, N.C. 51
Hilton Head 17
Hipps, Sen. Charles 67
Holden, Gov. W.W. 17
Hood, Gen. John B. 45
Hominy, N.C. 25
Hot Springs, N.C. 25
Huidekoper, F.W. 44
Hunsucker, Dan 47
Huntington, Collis P. 19

I

Illinois 17
Inman, John H. 44
Interstate Commerce Commission (ICC) 62, 63

J

Jackson County 29, 30, 64
Jackson County Economic Development Commission 61-64
Jackson Paper Co. 61
Jarretts 30
Jarrett House 51
Jarvis, Lt. Gov. Thomas J. 24
Johnson, President Andrew 17

K

Kanawha Hardwood Co. 74
Kentucky 40
Kephart, Horace 24

Killian's Kniting Mill 29
King, Judge Mitchell 12
Kitchen Lumber Co. 75
Knoxville, Tn. 34, 53

L

Lincoln, President Abraham 14, 17
Littlefield, Gen. Milton 17-19
Little Tennessee River 105-108
Logan, Thomas M. 24, 25
Love, Robert 79
Love, W.B. 78
Luthers 25
Lynchburg, Va. 16

M

MacNeill, Joan 66, 68
MacNeill, Malcolm 40, 66-70
Macon, Ga. 99
Maine 73
Marble, N.C. 80
Marietta & North Georgia R.R. 24, 34, 53
Martin, Gov. James 64-68, 110
Marion, N.C. 53
Massie, Tom 64
McBee, Vardry E. 27
Mead Paper Co. 60, 61
Medford, W. Clark 28, 49, 52
Melrose, N.C. 53
Memminger, Christopher 15
Memphis, Tn. 17
Mexico, Gulf of 52
Michigan 73
Mitchell County 52
Mitchell, Isaac 44
Mooney, James 12
Morehead, Gov. John Motley 14
Morgan, J.P. 45
Morgan, Sara Posey 88-91
Morganton 15, 16
Murphy Branch 1, 3, 13, 23, 46-52, 60-62, 74, 75, 82, 87
Murphy, N.C., 12, 32-35, 48, 50, 62-69, 78, 81

N

Nantahala Gorge 30-34, 47, 62, 71, 74, 87-89, 92-96, 104
Nantahala Mountains 4, 32
Nantahala, N.C. 30, 79, 81
N.C. Dept. of Transportation (DOT) 63, 70
N.C. General Assembly 13, 18, 24, 63, 67, 110
N.C. Railroad 14, 15
Newfound Gap 50, 75
New York 4, 68, 73

Nobel, Alfred 88
Nocona, N.C. 53
Noland, N.C. 55, 60, 101, 104, 106
Norfolk Southern R.R. 3, 49, 61-70, 75, 80-87, 96
Norfolk, Va. 24, 46
Norfolk & Western R.R. 46, 49, 61, 69, 80, 87
NRHS, Asheville Chapter 82
Northern Pacific R.R. 69
Norwood Lumber Co. 105

O

Old Fort 20, 21, 27, 34, 37, 78, 88, 89

P

Paint Rock 12, 13, 21, 24, 25, 27, 53
Parker & Reichman 67
Parris, John 39, 48, 88
Pennsylvania 73
Pigeon River 27, 28, 78
Pigeon River Gorge 31, 40
Pisgah National Forest 75
Philadelphia 4
Plott Balsams 29
Poinsett, Joel 12, 13
Proctor, N.C. 55, 60, 74, 104
Provost, R.W. 34

Q

R

Raleigh 17, 18
Ramsey, Rep. Liston 67
Ransom, Sen. 79
Redford, Robert 69
Red Marble Mountain 30-34, 71, 81, 85, 94
Reems Creek 25
Reichman, Andrew 67
Rhodo 34, 79, 81
Rhodo Tunnel 34, 35
Richmond & Danville R.R. 3, 15, 30, 35, 43-46, 80, 92
Richmond & West Point Terminal Co. 43, 44
Ridgecrest 37, 53, 88
Ritter, N.C. 104, 106
Ritter, W.M. Lumber Co. 74, 104, 105
Round Hill 103, 108
Russell, D.S.
Russell, Gov. D.L. 46

S

Salisbury, N.C. 14, 15, 24, 53, 78
Saluda, N.C. 49, 50, 53
Sandlin, Will Jr. 31, 32, 33, 34, 87-95, 101, 110
Sandlin, Will Sr. 31, 32, 88, 89
Santeetlah Creek 74
Sawyer, Joe 83
Saylor, Charles 85
Scott's Creek 29, 47
Scott, Bob 65, 66
Scruggs, Dr. 79
Seaboard Air Line R.R. 68, 69
Sherman, Gen. William T.
Shiloh 17
Slickrock Creek 75
Smoky Mountain Parkway 30
Smoky Mountain R.R. 104
Snowbird Lumber Co. 92
Southern Railway System 3, 40-61, 74-80, 85-104
Spartanburg, S.C. 52, 53, 86
Spencer, Lambert 44
Spencer, Samuel 44
Springfield, Ill., 17
Statesville, N.C. 50
Stoneman, Gen. George 15
Stroud, Steve 65, 66
Sullivan, Mark 63, 65
Sunburst, N.C. 75
Swain Co. 30, 64, 70
Swannanoa Gap 21, 37
S.W. Planning Commission 62, 64
Swepson, George 17-19
Sylva, N.C. 30, 60, 105
Syracuse, N.Y. 17

T

Talahassee Power & Light Co. 106
Taylor & Crate Lumber Co. 74
Tennessee 12
Tennessee, University of 96
Tennessee Valley Authority (TVA) 54, 60, 74, 83, 106, 107
Thomas, Sen. Royce "Bo" 67
Thomas, Col. William H. 12, 79
Topton, N.C. 30, 32, 81, 89, 90, 97, 104
Transylvania County 52, 53, 95
Tryon, N.C. 31
Tsali 56
Tuckasegee River 23, 37, 38, 71, 104
Turner, William P. 15
Twenty-Mile Creek 75

U

Union Pacific R.R. 69
U.S. Forest Service 106

V

Vance, Gov. Zebulon 20, 24, 79

W

Walker, Capt. Rufus 25, 25
Ward, Capt. A.E. 29
Warrior Mountain 31
Washington, D.C. 4, 108
Waynesville, N.C. 29, 66, 70
Welch, Manus 79
Wesser, N.C. 30, 54, 55, 61, 89, 104
West Buffalo Creek 74
Western & Atlantic R.R. 53
Western North Carolina Railroad 3, 11, 16, 25, 37, 41, 78
Whiting, F.S. Lumber Co. 74, 75
Whittaker, Steve 34
Whittier, N.C. 30, 48, 50
Wilmot, N.C. 48
Wilson, Major James 20, 27, 79
Winding Stairs 94
Winston-Salem 16, 82
Wood, Natalie 69

X

Y

Z